If we are not helping students to become confident, habitual readers, I don't know what business we are in.

The Book in Question

WHY AND HOW
READING IS IN CRISIS

Carol Jago

HEINEMANN
Portsmouth, NH

Heinemann

361 Hanover Street

Portsmouth, NH 03801–3912

www.heinemann.com

Offices and agents throughout the world

The author and publisher wish to thank those who have generously given permission to reprint borrowed material:

Cover image from *The Inexplicable Logic of My Life* by Benjamin Alire Saenz. Copyright © 2017 by Benjamin Alire Saenz. Published by Clarion Books, an imprint of Houghton Mifflin Harcourt Publishing Company.

Credits continue on page vi.

Library of Congress Cataloging-in-Publication Data

Name: Jago, Carol, author.

Title: The book in question : why and how reading is in crisis / Carol Jago.

Description: Portsmouth, NH : Heinemann, [2018] | Includes bibliographical references.

Identifiers: LCCN 2018015220 | ISBN 9780325098685

Subjects: LCSH: Reading (Middle school). | Reading (Secondary).

Classification: LCC LB1632 .J35 2018 | DDC 418/.40712—dc23

LC record available at https://lccn.loc.gov/2018015220

Editor: Sue Paro

Production Editor: Patty Adams

Cover Design: Suzanne Heiser

Cover Image: © Catherine McBride/Getty Images

Author Photograph: Andrew Collings

Interior Design: Monica Ann Crigler

Typesetter: Valerie Levy, Drawing Board Studios LLC

Manufacturing: Steve Bernier

Printed in the United States of America on acid-free paper

22 21 20 19 18 PAH 1 2 3 4 5

To my mother, Mary Crosetto, who suggests you read
Wislawa Szymborska's *Poems: New and Collected, 1957–1997*

CONTENTS

CHAPTER 1: The Problem *1*

Young people are losing the habit of reading. It is tempting to blame social media, video games, and the ubiquitous smartphone, but maybe teachers have not made a strong enough case for the importance of reading.

CHAPTER 2: Any Given Monday *15*

Every day teachers make 1,001 decisions, large and small, a few of which have the potential to change students' lives. Rethinking our approach to reading standards may help us make better decisions about what to teach and how to teach.

CHAPTER 3: Stimulating Competent, Confident, and Compulsive Readers *25*

Along with teaching students to read, we need to create classroom environments where students read widely and often, both under the direction of a teacher and on their own, for information and for pleasure.

CHAPTER 4: Teaching with Intention and Heart *36*

When teachers talk about rigor and relevance, the terms are sometimes falsely construed as opposites. We continue to read classical texts because they're relevant to contemporary readers. Good teaching focuses on perennial themes while supporting readers as they navigate textual challenges.

CHAPTER 5: Words, Words, Words *48*

Vocabulary instruction consumes enormous swathes of instructional time, often without significantly improving comprehension. Help students develop a love and respect for language by meeting words in their proper context—in books.

CHAPTER 6: Instructional Moves That Matter

Our approach to instruction can either encourage or discourage students from taking interpretive risks. Strengthen students' reading muscles through rhetorical readings of visual texts. Help them understand how a text creates a path to comprehending what it means.

CHAPTER 7: Losing Our Literature?

Including nonfiction in the curriculum need not result in the abandonment of literature. Create lessons that invite students to read a bouquet of texts, anticipating where young readers are likely to have difficulty and providing just-in-time scaffolding.

CHAPTER 8: Grasping Poetry

All too commonly, poetry is taught in one of two ways: (1) teacher chooses a poem she likes, reads it to the class, and asks students to identify the theme, or (2) teacher assigns students to write haikus. This chapter offers ideas for helping students read and take pleasure in their reading of poetry.

CHAPTER 9: Asking Better Questions

Good questions send students back to a text to reexamine and reflect upon what it means. They invite inquiry, opening up a passage for discussion from a range of perspectives. This chapter helps you compose evocative questions for the works you teach.

CHAPTER 10: Creating a Community of Readers

Teaching students to be self-motivated, independent learners should be our goal. Teenagers should leave our classrooms with a passion for learning and an insatiable desire to know more, see more, and read more.

Introduction

In conversations with colleagues I often hear the same complaint: students don't read anymore. *The Book in Question* is my attempt to address this alarming issue—alarming for teachers and even more terrifying for society.

Why don't teenagers read? It is tempting and fashionable to blame social media, video games, and the ubiquitous smartphone, but maybe we teachers are also at fault. In our urgency to prepare students to be "college and career ready," too often we turn what should be an intellectually stimulating reading assignment into a pointless chore. While strategy instruction can help make transparent to struggling readers what good readers do instinctively, it can also substitute a series of robotic steps for what reading actually is: an act of discovery.

I don't pick up a book in search of buried treasure, yet often that is what I find: nuggets of gold about what it means to be human, what it has meant to be human in the past, and what it might mean to be human in the future. After fifty years of reading, I'm still astounded by how much I don't know and how much books have to teach me. Though somewhat cowardly when it comes to taking risks in my own life, I'm an intrepid reader. I'll try anything.

Early in my teaching career, Steve Chesne, a seventh grader, challenged me, saying that I was always telling the class what to read but never asking students what I should read. "Fair enough," I thought. He came to school the next day with Arthur C. Clark's *Childhood's End*. This compelling story about overlords from outer space taking over the earth propelled me into months of reading science fiction, a genre that until that moment had never appealed to me. As middle school students love to do, Steve challenged me, and I thanked him for the challenge. Without his prodding, I might never have explored this genre. Notwithstanding the loss to my own reading life, I would also have been much less adept at recommending science fiction to future students. *Childhood's End*, along with William Gibson's *Neuromancer* and Orson Scott Card's *Ender's Game*, acquired a place of pride in my readers' circle collections.

In his opening essay to the Spring 2017 issue of *Lapham's Quarterly*, Lewis Lapham describes his own voyage of discovery as a reader.

> I live in all the pasts present on the page, and I begin to understand what the physicists have in mind when they talk about the continuum of time and space. . . . The stories that bear a second reading are those in which the author manages to get at the truth of what he or she has seen, felt, thought, knows, can find language to express. The task is never easy, but it is the labor of the writer's observation turned by the wheel of the reader's imagination that seeds the fertile ground . . . from which mankind gathers its common stores of energy and hope. (17–18)

I worry that if the next generation fails to acquire the reading habit, mankind's store of energy and hope will diminish and that we will find ourselves increasingly vulnerable. As A. E. Housman warned, in life, "luck's a chance, but trouble's sure" (1896). The truth of this observation was brought home to me while reading Angie Thomas' remarkable young adult novel *The Hate U Give* (2017). The book's sixteen-year-old protagonist, Starr Carter, has lost two friends to gun violence: one to a drive-by shooting, the other at the hands of the police, both in her presence. As Starr grapples with the responsibility of bearing witness—to a grand jury as well as to her own community—she demonstrates how it feels like to come of age in a society where prejudice is entrenched. Thomas' story contributes to our store of energy and hope by insisting on telling truth to power.

Reading books like *The Hate U Give* can change lives. Such books invite naturally solipsistic youth to consider how their own welfare is linked to the welfare of others. Worthwhile books challenge conventional assumptions and offer examples of how individual acts can alter the course of lives and even the course of history.

I want students to feel uneasy if they don't have something in line to read next. I want them to be so hungry for what they find in books that they read long into the night, avoid company, and even at times ignore their teacher.

This is not to say that young readers don't need teachers to guide them. Sometimes all they need is an enticing introduction to a story. Sometimes a lurid cover will hook them. At other times I need to accompany students on their journey through a book, helping them situate themselves in time and place and negotiate complicated syntax. It's a delicate balance. I want students to know what to do when their comprehension breaks down.

The most common reading "strategy," the one you and I use every day of our lives, is rereading. We slow down and read the sentence a second or third time. We pay attention to punctuation; we check if there is a word we misread or don't know. Making sense of complex text doesn't require a fancy acronym. All it needs is the desire to understand and the will to persevere.

But how does a teacher inspire students to want to understand *Beowulf* or *Othello?* And why should a student persevere through such unfamiliar textual worlds anyway? Wouldn't it be easier simply to assign Benjamin Alire Sáenz's remarkable book *The Inexplicable Logic of My Life*? That course would be easier but also pointless. We can't afford to waste instructional time teaching books that teenagers can, should, and will read on their own. English teachers frequently ruin such great stories for students by talking about foreshadowing and symbolism or by making students annotate the text and write an essay on character development. Is this what you look forward to doing after finishing a good book? I doubt it.

Only literary snobs read nothing but classics. I want students to range widely, pleasing as well as challenging themselves. My own reading life is wildly eclectic. I love nothing better than a Daniel Silva thriller to make a long airplane ride disappear. I also delight in contemporary classics like Anthony Marra's *Constellation of Vital Phenomena* and *The Tsar of Love and Techno*, which challenge me as a reader, taking me to places I've never been and immersing me in history I never knew, in this case the history of Chechnya. Marra's novels can be hard to follow. They force me to slow down, reread, and pay attention to every textual clue the author sows in order to keep track of events and characters. After finishing one of his books I long to talk about them with other readers. I know I will understand them better after hearing what others have seen and thought.

Filling in graphic organizers keeps students busy doing something you can observe. Thinking takes place out of sight. Instead of assigning artificial tasks for students to perform as they read, we should model our reading lessons after the way we read. This approach stands a good chance of both fostering a love of reading and building students' confidence in their own reading skills.

There is urgency to this work. In a world that has become increasingly polarized, stories invite readers to empathize with people who appear at first as The Other. Crossing such borders may entail discomfort and require navigation between the Scylla of unfamiliar settings and the Charybdis of unpronounceable character names. But this is a bridge to somewhere—to a more empathetic world.

CHAPTER 1

The Problem

I do believe books can change lives and give people this kind of language they wouldn't have had otherwise.

—Jacqueline Woodson

First the good news: in 2016, high school graduation rates rose to an all-time high of 83 percent. The bad news: many of these diploma holders do not read well enough to function in academic postsecondary education. While students are enrolling in college at record-setting rates, an estimated 40 percent are required to enroll in remedial course work, delaying and often ultimately preventing many from earning a degree. According to research by Education Reform Now (Barry and Dannenberg 2016), remedial classes are costing families 1.7 billion dollars each year. One of the most startling findings in the report is that the need for remedial education is not confined to low-income students. Students from middle- and high-income families are also arriving on campus underprepared for college work.

The California State University system had been offering placement exams and assigning students to remedial writing classes on the basis of these assessments for many years when instructors in writing programs began to notice a direct correlation between students' inability to express themselves and their inadequate comprehension of what they read. It is hard to write about a passage that you do not understand.

As the title *Out of Pocket: The High Cost of Inadequate High Schools and High School Student Achievement on College Affordability* suggests, the authors of the Education Reform Now study blame high school curriculum and instruction. They have a point, but I believe preparation for advanced study begins much earlier. Teenagers who were avid child readers tend to thrive at university. Why? They possess large vocabularies. They have a broad understanding of history, geography, and different cultures. They are confident in their ability to navigate dense syntax. Students fail to thrive in college largely on account of their fear of complex text. They lack confidence as readers. They don't have the stamina to persevere through information-laden material. Building that stamina takes years of reading and devoted care from teachers who know when to push and when to hold back and let the call of stories do some of the work for them.

True Grit

Research by Carol Dweck on growth mind-sets (2007) and Angela Duckworth on academic perseverance, or "grit," (2016) has influenced professional development all over the country. Schools, particularly those where students have traditionally underperformed, are attempting to teach these noncognitive skills. Students participate in grit skits, fill out practice grit worksheets, and even wear T-shirts displaying catchy phrases like, "Got Grit?" The results of these efforts—despite enormous grit on the part of teachers and consultants—are not encouraging. Despite hours of intervention classes teaching students how to cultivate a growth mind-set and develop academic perseverance, it appears that grit can't be taught the way we might teach *Life of Pi* or a lesson on photosynthesis.

There are, however, classrooms where students behave in gritty ways. What sets apart these classrooms where students demonstrate academic perseverance? C. Kirabo Jackson (2014), an economist at Northwestern University, tracked ninth-grade students in the state of North Carolina and found that classroom environment

had a significant impact on students' ability to deal with
setbacks and frustrations. Teachers who established
classroom communities where it was safe to take interpretive risks and that provided pathways for students
to correct their errors and redo shabby work fostered
academic resiliency. Students in these classrooms were
not learning new skills. They were learning how to think
and behave in new ways, ways that would serve them
well in academia and beyond.

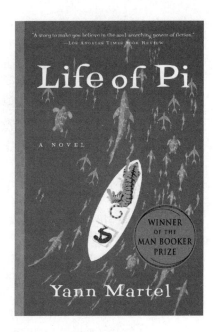

The generation of research inspired by Dweck and
Duckworth argues that grit resides not in the student as
an abiding character trait but in the context. The same
child who demonstrates remarkable pertinacity in math
class might give up at the first sight of a long novel. A
middle school student who showed notable academic
perseverance in eighth grade can suddenly feel hopeless
and helpless in high school.

The University of Chicago Consortium on School
Research conducted a study titled *Teaching Adolescents to Become Learners: The Role of
Noncognitive Factors in Shaping School Performance*, which concludes,

> Our review shows that academic behaviors have the most immediate
> effect on students' course grades. In relation to behaviors, much of
> the recent attention to noncognitive factors focuses on the idea of
> developing students' "grit" or perseverance in challenging work.
> However, despite the intuitive appeal of this idea, there is little
> evidence that working directly on changing students' grit or per-
> severance would be an effective lever for improving their academic
> performance. While some students are more likely to persist in tasks
> or exhibit self-discipline than others, all students are more likely to
> demonstrate perseverance if the school or classroom context helps
> them develop positive mindsets and effective learning strategies.
> In other words, the mechanisms through which teachers can lead
> students to exhibit greater perseverance and better academic
> behaviors in their classes are through attention to academic
> mindsets and development of students' metacognitive and self-
> regulatory skills, rather than trying to change their innate tendency
> to persevere. (Farrington et al. 2012, 8)

Time to toss the gritty worksheets. (If you think I am making this up, just search Google images for "grit worksheets.") Instead, help students build stamina for reading by reading. The muscles we use every day are the ones that become strong.

Achievement Is Driven by Interest

I have become increasingly wary of using "college readiness" as a motivational mantra. However many college banners we display in school hallways and college days we sponsor, some students find the idea of doing well in school as preparation for doing more school absurd if not repugnant. When asked, "Miss, why do we have to read this?" I am duty bound to offer a better answer than "Because I said so" or "Because you'll lose twenty points if you don't." The text and task should hold intrinsic value for the reader.

Students ascribe value to what interests them. Again and again I have seen achievement driven by interest. Students are much more willing to persevere with a long, complex text if they care about what it contains or when they have immediate use for the information presented. I'm not suggesting that we should pander to students' interests in popular culture but rather to expand their range of interests to topics they never imagined would appeal to them.

I never knew I was interested in the history of football until I read Steve Sheinkin's *Undefeated: Jim Thorpe and the Carlyle Indian School Football Team* (2017). Did you know that in football's early days, players on the field could punch one another? So many young men were seriously injured—a few even died—that a delegation of coaches approached President Theodore Roosevelt, a great lover of football from his days at Harvard, to tighten the rules of the game. They worried that unless administrative action was taken, football would be banned nationwide. As a result of the president's intervention, new rules of engagement and safety were implemented and the game opened up by the institution of the forward pass (Neff, Cohen, and Korch 1994).

It would be hard to find a reader who cared less about sports than me, yet Steve Sheinkin caught my attention and held it firm. He taught me things I didn't know I wanted to learn. Spellbound by the story of Jim Thorpe's life, I acquired information both necessary for understanding the events being described in the biography and useful for my own knowledge, information I would never in a million years have chosen to read about in *The Football Encyclopedia* (Neff, Cohen, and Korch 1994).

This kind of occurrence is common for avid readers. A student will pick up a book with an attractive cover, for example, Jackson Ntirkana and Wilson Meikuaya's *The Last Maasai Warriors: An Autobiography* (2016), and without necessarily intending to, begin learning all kinds of things about the Maasai's vanishing way of life on the African savannah and how two remarkable individuals are attempting to preserve that disappearing culture while helping their people find a place in the contemporary world. The coming-of-age ritual of slaying a lion may have been what drew the reader to the book initially, but by the time the student has turned the last page, his or her world has opened wider.

Serendipitous Reading

Serendipitous reading can be surprisingly informative. Though guided by no syllabus, a reader's life often has its own inner compass and inner logic. To help track this journey I ask students to keep a list of the books they read. The only require-ment is to record the book title, author, and date read. Don't you wish you had a list of all the books you read from ages ten to twenty? Wouldn't those titles paint a fascinating picture of what you were thinking and learning, of who you were?

Serendipitous reading works best with the help of teachers, librarians, and friends offering book recommendations. As a teenager I didn't know any other readers and never thought to ask for suggestions from others. I didn't think that's what one did. As a teacher, I try to make talking about books a natural part of every day's agenda. Call me a cockeyed optimist, but I believe that students who say they hate to read simply haven't yet found a book they like. My job is to find creative ways to put scores of books in students' paths and trust that one or two will pique their interest.

Because serendipitous reading is ignited by personal interest, the student is in control. Don't like this book? Pick up another. Confident readers feel no guilt at putting down a book that has lost its momentum. They don't feel that there is something wrong with the book or worry that there might be something wrong with their own reading skills. It is simply not the right book for right now.

Defining what makes a book just right is nearly impossible. For young children learning to read, the book's vocabulary and syntactical complexity clearly figure into the mix. But even a perfect readability match doesn't come close to capturing what it is that makes a particular text magical for a reader. I discovered *A Wrinkle in Time* as a ninth grader, relatively late to come to Madeline L'Engle's (2012) novel. The story captured my imagination, possibly because my mother had just had a baby and my feelings toward a much younger sibling seemed to be echoed in the main character's relationship with her small brother, Charles Wallace. Whatever it was, I was enraptured.

Neil Gaiman argues that "stories you read when you're the right age never quite leave you. You may forget who wrote them or what the story was called. Sometimes you'll forget precisely what happened, but if a story touches you it will stay with you, haunting the places in your mind that you rarely ever visit. Fantasy gets into your bones" (2007, 1). *A Wrinkle in Time* certainly got into mine, becoming a staple in my classroom library, often borrowed and much loved. Which was why a few years ago I decided to reread it. To my great surprise and disappointment, I was bored. All I could think of was that I was no longer the right age for the book to be just right for me. My younger brother, after all, had just turned fifty.

Choosing Books

Confident readers know how to choose books. Which is not to say that we are immune to error. Every avid reader I know has experienced book droughts where nothing you pick up has what you are looking for (not that you can articulate what you are looking for, but whatever it is, this isn't it). Students can fall into the same kind of reading funk, discarding dozens of books after only a few pages, rejecting every one of your surefire suggestions. When this happens, I ask students to write me a note describing the books they have rejected and explaining why they were disappointed. Complaints are welcome. Reflecting on their own decision making helps to jumpstart their reading engines. The notes also offer clues for me as to what is going on inside the young readers' heads.

Once on a class visit to the library to select books for independent reading, I watched as students milled about the room, strolling up and down the aisles, chatting cheerfully with one another, happy to be out of their desks. As various groups sensed my approach, they would randomly grab a book from the nearest shelf. I wasn't fooled. Neither was I satisfied with the vague task I had set. We could all do better.

The next time I scheduled a library visit, we prepared for it by discussing what students planned to look for in the stacks. Some had favorite authors whose additional books they wanted to read; others were interested in a particular genre, for example, graphic novels or fantasy. We talked about how to go about finding what they were looking for. We made a list of ten books that students thought others in the class would enjoy. As students talked, I took notes. The next day I handed out copies of my notes to students as they walked through the library doors. This time, along with stretching their legs, students selected their books with much greater intention.

Choosing books also requires a certain courage. I want students to have the confidence to follow their instincts and to take risks with books. I never discourage a student from a title because I think it may be too difficult; if it is, the reader will discover this soon enough. There are plenty of history books on our shelves at home—Charles Moore's multivolume biography of Margaret Thatcher and Robert Caro's four-volume biography of Lyndon Johnson, for example—that are too difficult or maybe just too long and detailed for me. An important step toward becoming a habitual reader is exploring the boundaries of your reading tastes.

A Book Pass

Another method for exposing students to a large number of books in a short amount of time is the book pass. I'm sure I learned about this from another teacher but have long forgotten from whom. If it was you, I apologize and hereby offer credit. Original ideas in teaching are few and far between. We steal, share, and pass along anything we find that works. Take it. What's mine is yours.

To prepare for this activity you need about three times as many books as you have students. The wider the variety of titles, the better: novels, biographies, poetry, graphic novels, memoirs, comedies, and tragedies. Make sure there is also a wide range of difficulty represented in the pile. Randomly place a book on every student's desk and tell the students they have one minute to peruse the book and either pass it on or hold onto it for possible reading later. Quickly offer students who have chosen to retain a book another one to pass along. After a few passes, call for a time-out to talk about how students are making decisions about books to read. Did they check out the author's picture? What could they tell from the covers? Did the opening sentences intrigue them? Was the book jacket summary enticing? Does length matter? How much? Let students know that you hope they will find a book that seems promising over the course of the next ten book passes.

I never insist that everyone select a book because, for one thing, a reader may already be in the middle of a spellbinding read. My goal is to expose students to books they may otherwise never handle and to increase their familiarity with the process of browsing books. Avid readers possess a whole set of habits of which they are mostly unaware and which they don't know how they acquired. I want to help every student develop as many of these book-browsing habits as possible. The activity also sends the message that we are all readers here, and that readers are always in search of their next good book.

Why All the Bad News?

On occasion I receive calls from parents, complaining—mostly gently, but complaining nevertheless—that the books their children are reading are too depressing. It is hard to argue that a thematic collection titled "Man's Inhumanity to Man" that includes Elie Wiesel's *Night*, John Hersey's *Hiroshima*, Mark Mathabane's *Kaffir Boy: The True Story of a Black Youth Coming of Age in Apartheid South Africa*, Francisco Jiménez's *The Circuit: Stories from the Life of a Migrant Child*, Richard Wright's *Black Boy*, and Michelle Alexander's *The New Jim Crow: Mass Incarceration in the Age of Colorblindness* is going to be an upbeat experience. After thanking these parents for caring about what their children read and for picking up the phone to query the selection, I try to make the case that "depressing" books help students put their own troubles in perspective. Admittedly the stories are dark, but young readers draw courage and inspiration from characters who have overcome extraordinary hardships. To quote Neil Gaiman once more, "Fairy tales are more than true: not because they tell us that dragons exist, but because they tell us that dragons can be beaten" (2012, 28). Compelling accounts of individuals confronting real-life monsters help students grow.

I don't mean to understate the extent of real trauma that many students are living through. But reading about how others have grappled with formidable obstacles can offer hope and inspiration. In the course of talking about a book, students reflect upon and sometimes open up about what lurks in the shadows of their own lives. *Michael Rosen's Sad Book* is a remarkable picture book illustrated by Quentin Blake. With great simplicity and a touch of humor, Rosen describes his feelings in the aftermath of his son's death. ("Sometimes I'm sad and don't know why. It's just a cloud that comes along and covers me up" (8)). The book offers readers permission to be sad and—without being in any way didactic—offers suggestions for healing.

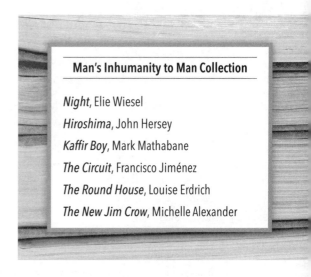

Man's Inhumanity to Man Collection

Night, Elie Wiesel

Hiroshima, John Hersey

Kaffir Boy, Mark Mathabane

The Circuit, Francisco Jiménez

The Round House, Louise Erdrich

The New Jim Crow, Michelle Alexander

I don't blame parents for wanting to surround their children with happy stories about happy families leading happy lives. That's their job. Mine is to offer stories that span the full range of human experience.

Volume Matters: Students Who Read Become Better Readers

I love research that supports what I already believe. Survey results from the National Assessment of Educational Progress (NAEP) in reading for eighth and twelfth grades demonstrate what English teachers know in our hearts to be true: students who read become better readers than those who don't.

◆ Eighth graders who read five or fewer pages per day scored lower than those who read more pages in school and for homework. Twelfth graders who read at least six to ten pages per day in school and for homework scored higher than those who read five or fewer pages. (U.S. Department of Education 2009b)

◆ Eighth graders who read for pleasure almost every day scored higher than those who read for fun less frequently. Twelfth graders who read for pleasure almost every day scored higher than students who never or hardly ever read for fun. (U.S. Department of Education 2009c)

It is also interesting to note that eighth graders who reported having a class discussion about their reading at least once a week or once or twice a month scored higher than those who reported having class discussions a few times a year or never or hardly ever (U.S. Department of Education 2009a). Twelfth graders who reported having a class discussion at least once a week scored higher than those who reported having a class discussion once or twice a month, a few times a year, or never or hardly ever.

The implications of these NAEP findings are clear. If we hope to see improvement in reading achievement, students will need to read significantly more in many different contexts for a variety of purposes, including their own pleasure. Volume matters. We should be concerned about the large number of students who *don't* read every bit as much as we worry about those who can't.

I know what you are probably thinking. "But my students are glued to their screens 24/7. They say they don't have time to read." According to the 2015 Common Sense Media survey of over 2,600 young people nationwide (Rideout 2015), on any given day, American teenagers spend about nine hours consuming entertainment media: watching television, playing video games, using social media and the Internet, and listening to music. This does not include time spent online at school or for homework. These are the same students who say they don't have time to do thirty minutes of reading at home because they have after-school jobs, childcare responsibilities, soccer practice, or violin lessons. Students have the time. They are simply choosing to pursue avenues of interest other than reading.

Of particular concern is the survey's finding that "children from lower-income homes and black and Hispanic children spend far more time with media—especially screen media—than white children and children from higher- and middle-income homes" (Rideout 2015, 86). It's easy to speculate as to causes, much harder to posit alternative outlets for teenagers hungry for stimulation and connection.

If I have piqued your interest to know more, here's the URL for the complete Common Sense Census report. It includes many fascinating aspects of teen media use. www.commonsensemedia.org /sites/default/files/uploads/research /census_researchreport.pdf.

I was appalled to learn how often students are distracted while doing homework—watching TV, texting, listening to music. According to the study, most teenagers believe that this multitasking has no impact on the quality of their work. Can you hear me grinding my teeth?

Imagine this scenario: Annie is in her bedroom reading Chapter 8 of *The Great Gatsby*. By her side—because it is always by her side—is her smartphone. Soon it vibrates with an incoming text. Annie responds quickly and returns to her book, for she is a good student who always completes her reading homework. But even in that short interval Annie has fallen out of Fitzgerald's narrative spell and has to return to the top of the page or the beginning of the paragraph to start again. Ten more text messages arrive (for Annie is also very well liked and sociable) before she can finish the chapter. As a result of the many interruptions, her homework reading takes longer and seems harder.

It is not within a teacher's power to pry those cell phones from students' hands. We can, however, invite students to reconsider their beliefs about multitasking, particularly when engaged in challenging intellectual endeavors. Daniel Levitin explains in his book *The Organized Mind: Thinking Straight in the Age of Information Overload*:

> It takes more energy to shift your attention from task to task. It takes less energy to focus. That means that people who organize their time in a way that allows them to focus are not only going to get more done, but they'll be less tired and less neurochemically depleted after doing it. . . . Perhaps most important, multitasking by definition disrupts the kind of sustained thought usually necessary for problem solving and for creativity. (2014, 170)

I believe many of our students are neurochemically depleted by the pressures of performance on social media platforms. They invest an enormous amount of time and effort into constructing their online persona and maintaining their online presence. Is this time well spent? I'm not convinced that it is.

Perhaps suggest to students that as an experiment they put their cell phones in another room while doing homework for one night. They don't even have to turn the phones off, just put them out of earshot. Have students keep track of how long it takes to complete the reading without interruption or distraction. Any decision

> *I believe many of our students are neurochemically depleted by the pressures of performance on social media platforms.*

about how to work in the future is, of course, up to them. Teenagers hate being told what to do. They can, however, be persuaded to adopt a practice that saves both time and energy.

Reading Online and Off

Schools will in the near future likely become paperless places. Upon arrival, students will be handed devices preloaded with instructional materials and links to assigned readings. Books will be in evidence, but reading on screens will be the norm. What challenges will this brave new classroom pose for young readers?

Putting aside technological snafus, issues of bandwidth, and district filters, I'm interested in how reading may or may not be affected as we move from print on paper to pixels on a screen. Are there skills we should be teaching today to prepare students for reading tomorrow?

Research on screen reading tells us that skimming has become the norm. Ziming Liu (2012), a professor at San José State University, found that screen-based reading is characterized by browsing and scanning, keyword spotting, and nonlinear movement through the text. Online readers also demonstrate decreased sustained attention.

Before declaring Liu's findings the end of deep reading (and therefore civilization) as we know it, I have to confess that I've always tended to read too fast—both online and on the page—skimming texts that should be savored, skipping descriptive passages, and ignoring all graphs and charts. I try to persuade myself that what I miss in detail I make up in volume but have learned to discipline myself to slow down for complex text, particularly poetry and letters from government offices.

It may be that teachers are worrying too much about the difference between paper and screen and not enough about the differences entailed in various purposes for reading. Often research studies compare student comprehension of a story read on an e-reader with comprehension from a print version. But the measure of comprehension in these studies is often a series of multiple-choice questions. That's not how I would assess students' understanding of any book. Differences in performance on researchers' quizzes may have less to do with screen versus print than they do with the background knowledge readers bring to the story or students' engagement with the text.

There are few substantial differences between reading literature on an e-reader and reading a book. With most e-books there's nothing on the screen but print.

Once a reader becomes familiar with the device, even
those differences disappear. In an interesting development in the book versus e-book debate, a 2016 Nielsen
survey of book sales in Britain reported that e-book sales
had declined by four percent for the second consecu-
tive year. Are young people using books as a break from
their devices and social media? Could it be that students
themselves are beginning to balance their screen and
printed-page reading time?

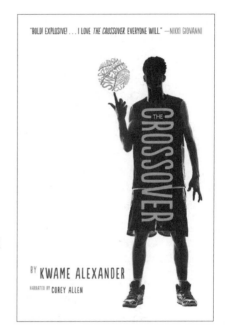

On the other hand it is important to draw students'
attention to the significant differences between reading
a book on a tablet and reading online news, articles, and
search results on a device. Online readers are bombarded
with competing images and text features. Hyperlinks
tempt the reader to stray from the continuous text. For
example, you can find an excellent article from the *New
Yorker* by Maria Konnikova (2014) called "Being a Better
Online Reader" at www.newyorker.com/science/maria-
konnikova/being-a-better-online-reader. If you were reading the book you have in
your hand online, you could go to the article immediately. But should you click on
the link now or later? And if you clicked now, do you think you'd return to this page?
Readers of online texts make such decisions all the time. Konnikova argues that the
online world "exhausts our resources more quickly than the page. We become tired
from the constant need to filter out hyperlinks and possible distractions."

I restrain myself from following any link to the *Huffington Post*. Why? Because
before I get halfway through the article I intended to read, I am lured to click on a
link to what some celebrity has done or said or is wearing. In the blink of an eye, an
hour has gone by with nothing to show for it—apart from the occasional new pair of
shoes. The article I originally linked to has been all but forgotten. Ask your students
to identify a website that commonly distracts them and for homework pinpoint what
it is on the site or about the site that causes them to spend so much time there. Your
resident gamers will particularly like being able to tell their parents, who find them
browsing the World of Warcraft website, that they are doing research.

One way to demonstrate how reading habits can differ from print to screen is
to find a compelling article from an online source and to print out the first page.
If possible, eliminate any markers that suggest this is an online text. Have students
read and annotate page one in print and then ask them to read the rest of the article

online. After they have finished, have students write for a few minutes about what they noticed in terms of their own comprehension, ease of reading, and retention of content. Use their responses as a springboard for a classroom discussion about reading online versus from a print source. The goal here is not to determine if one is better than the other but rather to tease out the differences in how we approach and process information presented online and how we behave with printed text.

It is important for students to understand their own vulnerability to technology. Multitasking is seductive as well as counterproductive to learning. Notifications alert us to incoming, occasionally important, messages, but they also distract us from the work at hand. In order to concentrate when I write, I have to quit all programs behind Microsoft Word. It's simply too tempting to slip away from the difficult task of constructing coherent sentences and check my Twitter feed.

Bemoaning the ubiquity of technology is pointless. Devices will become ever more present in all of our lives. The larger problem is that too many students are choosing not to read. As a result they are less informed, less articulate, and I believe less understanding of others. Reading is a path to the world around us: to foreign relations, car maintenance, human emotion.

Time to lead the way.

CHAPTER 2

Any Given Monday

*True literature only exists when it is created by madmen,
hermits, heretics, dreamers, rebels and skeptics; not
by reliable clerks just doing their jobs.*

Yevgeny Zamyatin

Teaching is exhausting. Not only because of the number of students one meets in a day or the number of papers one has to grade. More wearing is the sheer number of decisions we make per hour—per minute on some days. Should I call on Graham with his head down or should I let him be? Is he reflecting upon the sonnet we just read or is he snoozing? Should I ignore Samantha's eye roll or use it as an example of a microaggression that undermines the classroom community? If my instruction is failing, do I forge ahead according to my lesson plan or stop and query students on why they seem to be disengaged? No wonder that at day's end, teachers can barely stumble out to the parking lot.

Students, on the other hand, race from the school doors bursting with energy. Something's wrong with this picture. When the last bell rings, I want students to be dripping with sweat and not because the building's air conditioner is broken. I want them to be intellectually spent from all the thinking they have done. That, at least, is my goal.

It is easy to lose sight of one's goal, however. Let me state mine here in a single sentence. I want students, able to read and write well, to choose to read and write often. Simple. It is also much easier to remember than a long list of English language arts standards.

Standards: A Double-Edged Sword

I don't mean to denigrate standards. The movement to define standards delineates what we want students to know and be able to do. It has also unintentionally created a ceiling for achievement. True excellence in reading, writing, and thinking can't be prescribed. It is idiosyncratic and rarely develops evenly across the grades. Extraordinary performances sometimes depend on the wind of inspiration to blow in just the right direction for just the right amount of time. A standards-based curriculum that leaves no room for creativity is dangerously short-sighted.

I have always held that, given knowledgeable teachers, adequate textbooks, and clean, safe schools, most children can achieve proficiency. What I worry about is that, in the process of putting standards into practice in order to raise the level of student performance, we might also limit or circumscribe that performance. The last fifteen years of educational reform have, alas, proved me correct. The sensible plan to align assessment with standards became complicated, effectively distorted, when certain states made student test results a factor in teacher evaluation. In several districts, but particularly in low-performing schools, many hours of instructional time were given over to test preparation. Instead of pursuing the lofty performance levels described in the standards, teachers chased correct answers to sample multiple-choice items. For too many children, practice tests—not poetry—became the basis for their lessons.

I cannot help but be reminded of Matthew 16:26 (New American Standard Bible). "What will it profit a man if he gains the whole world and forfeits his soul?" For what will it profit our nation if we achieve 100 percent proficiency on assessments and forfeit students' passion for reading and writing?

The Girl Who Threw Butterflies for New York State

Assessment holds a place of pride in today's educational landscape. Although exams offer—at best—a snapshot of what students know and can do, test scores provide numbers for policy makers to conjure with. Hard data rule. As a longtime teacher and pragmatist, I make my peace with the beast by recognizing that while tests are only a proxy for performance, student results—particularly results from a well-designed assessment—offer insight into my own instruction and guidance for improvement.

Take, for example, the released items from the New York State Common Core assessment (NCS Pearson 2014). A seventh-grade English language arts item asks students to read an excerpt from a story by Mick Cochrane called "The Girl Who Threw Butterflies," about a young girl who joins the boys' baseball team. The story describes how "shouting didn't come easily to Molly" and how her coach Morales "teased her into it" (16). One reading comprehension item asks students to draw inferences from these details.

While all the choices are plausible, and in classroom discussion would be welcomed as part of our emerging understanding of the characters and their actions, A is clearly the best answer. If students had difficulty understanding why this was so, I would invite them to reread the passage and help them consider how "pushing her to develop skills she has never used before" was more specifically related to details in the story regarding Molly's soft-spoken nature and her coach's actions: "He cupped his ear like an old, hard-of-hearing man. 'Did someone say something?' Before long, Molly was hollering out instructions to her infielders loud and clear. She stopped worrying about sounding ladylike and concentrated on being heard" (16).

Is answering this kind of multiple-choice question an artificial task? Absolutely yes. But is it unreasonable to expect thirteen-year-old students to be able to complete such a task occasionally for the purpose of assessment? I think not.

The mistake too many schools make is to invest precious classroom time walking through such test items rather than having students read and talk about their reading. It breaks my heart to see cash-strapped campuses purchase test-prep materials instead of books. We need to help children develop an appetite for reading, a thirst for learning, and a hunger to talk about what they are thinking. We need to keep our eye on the ball. The goal should be an educated populace, not a nation of good test takers.

Voracious young readers who have knowledgeable, caring teachers to guide their reading selections in all likelihood possess a large vocabulary, broad background knowledge, and wide experience with text types. Those who read more, know more.

> Avid readers are
> intrepid, unafraid of
> archaic language and
> dense syntax.

And the more children learn from the books they consume, the less difficult they find the next book—or any exam text. Avid readers are intrepid, unafraid of archaic language and dense syntax. They understand that *long* doesn't necessarily equate with *boring* and know what to do when sentence structures become complex. Developing such readers won't happen overnight, but when we focus on developing readers, the tests students meet might challenge but will never defeat them.

I believe it is time to rethink our relationship with standards. Instead of using standards as a checklist for evaluating curriculum and instruction, let us employ them to instigate professional conversations with colleagues about teaching and text selection, lesson planning and writing tasks. Standards embody ideas that evolve over time. I know no one who has been involved in standards writing or standards review who, upon reflection, wouldn't want to revise one or two.

Take, for example, the eighth-grade Common Core State Standard for writing narratives (CCSS.ELA-LITERACY.W.8.3). "Write narratives to develop real or imagined experiences or events using effective technique, relevant descriptive details, and well-structured event sequences" (NGA Center for Best Practices and CCSSO 2010). That seems reasonable enough. But teaching to this standard became murky when Common Core test specifications determined that all writing should be "evidence-based." I understand the desire for consistency across the three writing types (informational, argumentative, and narrative). It seems to me, however, that to demand narrative writing be evidence-based is nonsensical. Are most stories not works of imagination tethered only tangentially to evidence? Of course a storyteller probably does engage in research for accuracy of detail, but to call the resulting product evidence-based makes no sense. My heart goes out to the poor item writers who have to produce coherent writing tasks to meet these test requirements.

More than anything else, I worry about the distortion of teaching for the sake of testing. It is not only the waste of instructional time but also the loss of spontaneity, edginess, and even eccentricity. Yevgeny Zamyatin wrote, "True literature only exists when it is created by madmen, hermits, heretics, dreamers, rebels and skeptics; not by reliable clerks just doing their jobs" (Radzinsky 1997, 57). Maybe the same is true for teachers. I don't really want madmen teaching children, but I see nothing wrong with dreamers and skeptics. Kids deserve better than reliable clerks just doing their jobs. And if teaching to standards results in more clerklike behavior on the part of teachers, maybe it is time to revise the standards. In a more radical move, what about going standards-free for a while? It is not as though teachers have no internalized standards about what they expect from their students.

Another approach might be to take more deeply to heart Common Core Anchor Standard 10 for reading (CCSS.ELA-LITERACY.CCRA.R.10). "Read and comprehend complex literary and informational texts independently and proficiently" (NGA Center for Best Practices and CCSSO 2010). That is a standard I applaud.

Curricular Risks

Clerks put compliance first. And while compliance can protect a teacher from criticism, it rarely results in inspired instruction. I would never tell students they have to read *To Kill a Mockingbird* because they have to. Much better to introduce Harper Lee's novel as a book you loved. If you have established a rapport with students, they will be curious to know why. And answers to that why begin on page one.

Compliance also leads to teaching in place. While I recognize that starting with a new set of texts every year is an unreasonable expectation—I need to teach a novel for three years before I am able to teach it well—changing things up can breathe new life into teaching. It's easy to become stale. And if you are bored with the text, students will sense it, and their complaints will magnify. I say this as someone who taught *Julius Caesar* for twenty-eight years in a row. Of course I only really taught the first three acts up through the funeral orations. I handled Acts IV and V, which are really quite dull apart from the closing speeches, by assigning them for homework over a weekend (I never kidded myself that everyone was completing the reading) and on Monday showed an excerpt from the 1953 Marlon Brando film beginning with Caesar's stroll to the Forum through to the end of the play.

Many of the other tenth-grade teachers in my department switched to *Macbeth*, but I chose to continue with *Julius Caesar* because I felt the funeral orations of Brutus and Marc Antony were perfect for rhetorical analysis as well as for memorization. I recoiled from the idea of teaching the orations out of context. I wanted students to see the rivals in action in order to understand why Shakespeare has them speak to the Roman crowd as they do.

If everyone in our English department had had to comply with a curriculum mandate requiring everyone to teach the same play, blood might have been spilt (not really, but you know how heated English teachers can be when it comes to their favorite books). Instead, we agreed that all tenth-grade students would read at least one Shakespeare play over the course of the year. While conversations about what to teach and when are essential for curricular coherence, enforcing strict compliance rides roughshod over teachers' natural individual preferences.

Compliance also leaves little room for risk taking. Before you accuse me of teaching in place, I should tell you that I made the commitment to myself to teach one new book every year. This kept me constantly on the lookout for new titles and fresh authors. It also kept me in search of funding for seventy new books every year. This was easier than I initially imagined. Small grants, PTSA funding, department budgets, and individual donors all helped out. Again and again I made the case in requests that we needed to refresh what we asked students to read. I would show potential donors Arthur Applebee's (1989) list of the most common books taught in high school and they would inevitably comment, "But those are the same books I read in high school!" Exactly.

How will we ever renew the set of staple texts that continue to be taught if teachers are reluctant to teach new titles? If the consensus across your middle school campus is that sixth graders are bored with Steinbeck's *The Pearl*, why not experiment with Linda Sue Park's *A Long Walk to Water*? Inspired by what they learn in this novel, based on a true story about the lost boys of Sudan and about access to clean water in Africa, students across the country are becoming involved with the nonprofit organization Water for South Sudan.

Book-Length Works Taught in High School English Classes (Research by Arthur Applebee)

The ten titles taught most frequently in public schools:

1. *Romeo and Juliet*
2. *Macbeth*
3. *Huckleberry Finn*
4. *Julius Caesar*
5. *To Kill a Mockingbird*
6. *The Scarlet Letter*
7. *Of Mice and Men*
8. *Hamlet*
9. *The Great Gatsby*
10. *Lord of the Flies*

If twelfth graders are grumbling about the absence of authors of color in their syllabus, assign them *Between the World and Me*, by Ta-Nehisi Coates. The author's argument, modeled on James Baldwin's "Letter to My Nephew" and written as a letter to his own fifteen-year-old son, is intentionally provocative, just the thing to combat the debilitating ennui of senior year. Only by experimentation will we ever know what else is possible.

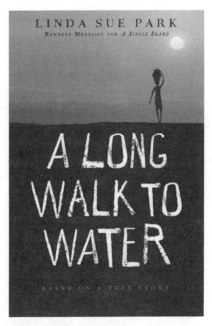

I don't want to pretend that every new book I introduced worked perfectly and remained in my curriculum forever. Sometimes after teaching a book I realized that the text would be better placed in another grade. Sometimes a book that I loved, like *Snow Falling on Cedars*, by David Guterson, or *The Bean Trees*, by Barbara Kingsolver, simply offered too little meat to be worthy of the investment of our instructional time. Students had no need of me when reading these books. Was the money I spent on copies wasted? Absolutely not. We simply moved the titles to our readers' circle lists and made use of them there. Both titles worked beautifully in student-run book clubs. Richard Wright's *Black Boy* and Amy Tan's *The Joy Luck Club*, on the other hand, became anchor texts in our tenth-grade core curriculum.

Here are some titles that I believe would be worth taking a risk with:

Middle School

Sachiko: A Nagasaki Bomb Survivor's Story, by Caren Stelson (nonfiction)

March: Book Three, by John Lewis, Andrew Aydin, and Nate Powell (graphic biography)

We Will Not Be Silent: The White Rose Student Resistance Movement That Defied Hitler, by Russell Freedman (nonfiction)

I, Too, Sing America: Three Centuries of African American Poetry, by Catherine Clinton (poetry)

My Seneca Village, by Marilyn Nelson (poetry)

The Distance Between Us (young readers edition), by Reyna Grande (memoir)

The Great American Dust Bowl, by Don Brown (graphic nonfiction)

Brown Girl Dreaming, by Jacqueline Woodson (memoir in verse)

Woods Runner, by Gary Paulsen (historical fiction with nonfiction interchapters)

Where the Mountain Meets the Moon, by Grace Lin (fiction)

Flesh and Blood So Cheap: The Triangle Fire and Its Legacy, by Albert Marrin (nonfiction)

Riot, by Walter Dean Myers (play)

Primates: The Fearless Science of Jane Goodall, Dian Fosse, and Biruté Galdikas, by Jim Ottaviani and Maris Wicks (graphic biography)

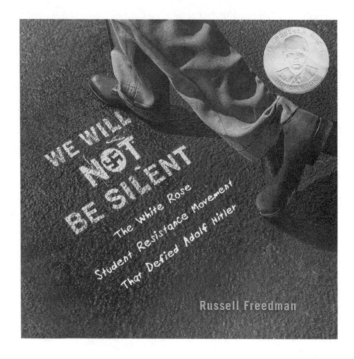

High School

Evicted: Poverty and Profit in the American City, by Matthew Desmond (nonfiction)

When Breath Becomes Air, by Paul Kalanithi (memoir)

Beyond Katrina: A Meditation on the Mississippi Gulf Coast, by Natasha Tretheway (memoir)

Exit West, by Mohsin Hamid (fiction)

The Piano Lesson, by August Wilson (play)

The Hour of Land: A Personal Topography of America's National Parks, by Terry Tempest Williams (nonfiction)

The Light of the World, by Elizabeth Alexander (memoir)

The Mersault Investigation, by Kamel Daoud (fiction)

Justice: What's the Right Thing to Do? by Michael Sandel (nonfiction)

All the Light We Cannot See, by Anthony Doerr (fiction)

My Life as a Foreign Country, by Brian Turner (memoir)

Billy Lynn's Long Halftime Walk, by Ben Fountain (fiction)

The Good Soldiers, by David Finkel (nonfiction)

The Crusades of Cesar Chavez, by Miriam Pawel (biography)

Behind the Beautiful Forevers: Life, Death, and Hope in a Mumbai Undercity, by Katherine Boo (nonfiction)

Lab Girl, by Hope Jahren (memoir)

It may have struck you that none of the books on the high school list was written especially for young readers. Neither were any of the books on Arthur Applebee's list of evergreen classics. My list also includes more nonfiction titles than typically appear in a middle or high school curriculum.

After a lifetime of reading almost nothing but fiction, I am enjoying nonfiction to a surprising extent. Writers like sociologist Matthew Desmond, whose book *Evicted* won the 2017 Pulitzer Prize for general nonfiction as well as the PEN/John Kenneth Galbraith Award and National Book Critics Circle Award, often make their argument through the use of narrative. Desmond supports his claim that chronic eviction is both a cause and result of poverty with the stories of tenants and landlords in urban Milwaukee. His ethnographic study describes in heartbreaking detail the physical and psychological toll insecure housing takes on families and communities. The book reads with all the immediacy of a novel.

On any given Monday teachers have a host of decisions to make: some curricular, some pedagogical, many emotional. Finding the balance between the expectations of standards and the particular needs of a particular group of students on a particular day is a constant challenge. And the importance of the choices we make is daunting. Young lives are at stake. What helps me remain sane amid all the variables is the knowledge that our work is not perfectible, that it will always be a work in progress. The lesson that sparkles in period 1 can fall flat in period 4. The book that inspires rich discussion and compelling student writing one year might flop the next. Let's observe, reflect, and revise in an ongoing cycle. Let's also give ourselves permission to fail. Those miserable Mondays can also be teachable moments.

CHAPTER 3

Stimulating Competent, Confident, and Compulsive Readers

Never trust anyone who hasn't brought a book with them.
—Lemony Snicket (aka Daniel Handler)

If English teachers are unable to convince students that it is valuable to lead a literate life—reading, engaging in conversations about books, thinking about the textual world—catastrophe looms. Anarchy threatens. Democracy is at risk. An exaggeration? Maybe. But the importance of working toward the goal of ensuring every child grows up to be an able and avid reader cannot be overstated. Circumscribing the content and quality of what we have students read deprives them of their literary rights. It is intellectually disenfranchising.

Teenagers' reading habits resemble their eating habits. Lured by intense marketing, many kids have become addicted to the sugar and salt in fast food, first forgetting and later disdaining fruit and vegetables. As a result, their health has declined, their ability to concentrate has diminished, and to no nutritionist's surprise, they seem always to be hungry. Applying a similar scenario to reading, teens have been sold the latest devices, social media platforms, and video games. Some teachers, keen to keep the curriculum relevant for digital addicts, invite students to write Twitter messages from Romeo to Juliet, reduce reading assignments to excerpts, and shy away from nineteenth-century authors. Textual nuggets have about as much nourishment as the chicken variety. As a result, students are intellectually starved. Though they may not recognize it themselves, they are hungry for better fare.

Healthy Reading

In *Secrets from the Eating Lab*, a study designed to help children learn to eat more healthily, Tracy Mann (2017) found that the surest, maybe the only, way to get kids to eat vegetables is to place the celery and carrots in a competition they can win: vegetables versus nothing. Using schoolchildren for their subjects, researchers conducted two field tests. In one, they placed carrots on students' plates along with the rest of their lunch. Most of the carrots were left untouched. According to the School Nutrition Association, over 70 percent of the fruit and vegetables in student lunches are discarded uneaten. In a second field test, they placed cups of carrots on cafeteria tables before students were allowed in line pick up their lunches. The result? Four hundred and thirty percent more carrots were consumed! When children are hungry and nothing else is on offer, they eat their vegetables.

I have to be careful not to push this comparison too far, as I don't want to suggest that English curriculum should consist solely of literary broccoli. But if given the choice between reading *The Scarlet Letter* and *The Hunger Games*, most students—including your good readers—would choose the latter. Admit it: most days, wouldn't you? But the books we teach shouldn't necessarily be those that slip down most easily. Texts worth studying, worth reading closely, do occasionally get stuck in a reader's throat. They challenge students' expectations of how the world works and what happens when it doesn't. They force readers to stretch and, in so doing, become better readers.

At the conclusion of her study, Tracy Mann suggests that it is easier to eat well when surrounded by people with healthy eating habits. Could this be a clue as to why students in honors and Advanced Placement classes often seem to make more progress than students in regular classes? Of course many other factors affect and determine student performance, but peer pressure has a powerful impact. When everyone around you disdains carbonated beverages and chooses an apple over a doughnut, you tend to make similar choices.

Parents at the high school where I taught often demanded their children be placed in honors classes even when counseled that their children were underprepared for the course work. Parents didn't care. They believed it was more important for their children to be surrounded by students who did the homework, behaved in class, and generally conformed than it was to earn an A. It's hard to argue with their thinking. I felt the same when my son attended Santa Monica High School. Clearly we had work to do as a department to establish the same norms in every class, but parents had a nose for where students were learning the most.

What about the effect of being surrounded by good books? Many students grow up in book deserts. In the same way that growing up in a food desert can determine which foods kids do and don't choose to eat, so limited access to books can affect students' attitudes toward reading. If it were within my power, I would give every English teacher three thousand dollars a year to stock their classroom libraries with fresh and nourishing books. I would provide every middle and high school with a clean, well-lighted library run by a knowledgeable librarian or two. I would ensure that every community had a five-star public library offering books in many formats for readers of every age. And I would reinstate traveling libraries to reach every child, no matter how remote their home.

A Culture of Reading

Alas, I do not possess such power. We are, however, in charge of what happens inside our classrooms. Our aim should be to ensure that every minute is packed with thinking, reading, writing, lots of talk, and lots of books. To that end we need to reexamine the assumption that students can read only one book at a time. Teachers tell me that they have a hard enough time getting students to read the text being studied let alone read a book outside class for pleasure. Is this congruent with calling the class college prep? Students will certainly have to read more than one book at a time in college. In addition, if students' only experience of reading is with a book that demands significant effort on their part to comprehend, they are unlikely ever to consider reading for the pleasure of it.

Students, particularly those who don't grow up in homes where parents or siblings read habitually, are often surprised to learn that people actually read by choice rather than by necessity. Luring students to a book-full life does not just happen. It requires determination and a plan. The first requirement is that the teacher be a reader. In every job interview I conducted as English department chair, I always asked, "So what are you reading?" or "If you could recommend one book to a ninth grader, what would it be?" I could tell a great deal about candidates' own reading lives from their answers. I was also confident that while the department could support a new teacher through the agonies of classroom management and grading policies, we were unlikely to turn someone who did not love to read into someone who did.

One way for teachers to demonstrate that they walk the walk is to institute an after-school book club. Santa Monica High School teachers learned a great deal about why we often disagreed on what to teach and how to teach as we talked about books. Gabriel García Márquez's *Love in the Time of Cholera*, Ruth Prawer Jhabvala's *Heat and Dust*, and Thomas Pynchon's *The Crying of Lot 49* challenged us to grapple with texts we ourselves didn't fully understand. These books also reminded us of the importance of literature in our own lives, reinvigorating our passion for reading challenging texts. A high point in the life of the book club was a cross-curricular afternoon with the social studies department discussing Cormac McCarthy's *Blood Meridian*. It was fascinating to see how different the history teachers' approach to reading the novel was from that of the English teachers. We often argued until dark over what to read next.

While a well-stocked classroom library and a passionate reader-teacher are critical ingredients of a vibrant reading program, they are not enough. You need to create a culture of reading within your classroom. Start by talking with students about books you love, books you could not put down, and books you think they might like. Let them know what kind of reader you were (or were not) when you were their age. I like sharing this story about myself as a reader:

> When I was ten years old, I was in the car taking my mother to the hospital to give birth to my youngest brother. Our route passed the library, and I was unreasonably (according to my father) insistent

that we stop so I could check out a book. I was adamant that they couldn't possibly leave me at the neighbor's house with nothing to read. My poor mother had to wait while I chose *The Life of Leif Erikson*. My family loves retelling the story as evidence of both my bossiness and social ineptitude. Without a book, I was lost.

I tell the story for a number of reasons. Students always prick up their ears when their teacher offers to reveal personal information. More importantly, I want to model how to talk about one's reading life and to demonstrate how reading helped me survive awkward moments and relieved the boredom of childhood. I have always been better at reading than at handling real life.

I then invite students to write for a few minutes about a book or storytelling memory from their own childhood. I have yet to teach a student who did not have one. We share these with partners and then together look for common themes, which I post as they emerge:

- being read to from a beloved storybook
- reading through a series they loved
- listening to a grandparent's stories
- discovering the first book they could read
- savoring their favorite book as a child
- reading a book that scared them

I ask students to title a new piece of paper "We Used To" and to write a short poem describing their own reading experiences as well as the experiences of others. I urge them to think about what they used to do and feel as readers when they were young. After about ten minutes, I tell students to create a new heading with the title "Now We." Below that title I invite students to write a companion poem describing themselves as readers today. When students ask if they can take this home to revise, I of course acquiesce. Quincy Troupe's poem "Flying Kites" (2002) provided me with the inspiration for this lesson. It works beautifully as a mentor text for students as they write their poems.

The lesson establishes that I care about students as readers and want to know more about their reading lives. I am curious about what they like and what they think they dislike about books. Intentionally omitted is any reference to reading levels or reading scores.

Book Talks

Successful book talks inspire students to want to read a particular book. They provide the yeast that makes enthusiasm for reading rise. When thinking about how to pitch a book to students, I look for something that will make them perk up their ears. For example:

- "*Fish Girl* is a graphic novel about a young mermaid held captive and put on display in a boardwalk aquarium."

- "Though Mohsin Hamid's novel *Exit West* portrays the future realistically, he includes one fantastical element: doors that allow refugees from war-torn countries to emerge magically in the West. It's also a love story exploring the meaning of refuge."

- "In Barbara Kingsolver's novel *The Bean Trees*, Taylor Greer's goal is to graduate from high school without getting pregnant."

- "You know Trevor Noah as the host of *The Daily Show*. What you might not know is that he grew up in South Africa under apartheid. The title of his memoir *Born a Crime* refers to the fact that his birth was the result of a crime. His father was white and his mother black."

- "Miriam Moss wrote *Girl on a Plane* based on her own experience of being on an airplane hijacked by terrorists when she was fifteen years old."

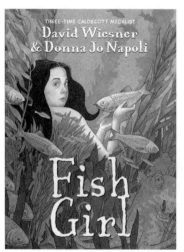

A good place to start when preparing a book talk is Amazon.com. Their plot summaries are written to make hitting that 1-Click ordering button irresistible—exactly the same thing I'm trying to accomplish in the classroom. The short vignettes also help me recall character names and plot details that lend texture to my book talk.

I learned most of what I know about composing effective book talks from my school librarian. Watching Mary Purucker recommend books to kids was a wonder to behold. The titles she talked about flew off her library shelves. Consider inviting your school librarian or someone from your local public library to book talk a dozen popular titles to your class. Take notes on how a professional captures the essence of a book without giving away too much. Two national masters of the book talk are Teri Lesesne and Donalyn Miller. If you ever have an opportunity to hear either of them speak, do not miss the chance. The experience is likely to strain your book budget, but you will come away inspired to read more.

A book talk can also be an occasion to warn students about aspects of a book that they or their parents might find troubling. With some titles, for example, J. M. Coetzee's *Disgrace*, I might ask students to obtain permission from home before checking out the book. Why should this be necessary for a book by a Nobel Laureate in literature? Because the novel was written for adult readers and the main character's behavior—David Lurie admits to a rape but shows no remorse—could be morally confusing for a seventeen-year-old reader. I feel the same way about Vladimir Nabokov's *Lolita*. Including parents in conversations about the books students are choosing to read is not censorship but common sense.

The book talks that have the greatest effect, of course, are those given by other students, especially popular kids not particularly known for their love of books. It helps to offer a few guidelines:

- ◆ Your goal is to entice others in the class to want to read your book.
- ◆ Aim for a three-minute presentation.
- ◆ You may read from the book for up to one minute.
- ◆ Have the physical book in hand or the cover image on a PowerPoint slide.
- ◆ Do not give away the ending.
- ◆ Repeat the title and author at the conclusion of your talk.
- ◆ Practice with a partner before delivering your book talk.

Listening to thirty-six student book talks in a row can be extremely tedious and even counterproductive. I try to spread the talks out over the course of a grading period, listening to three or four every week. My objective is to provide the class with a constant stream of book recommendations from their peers. The only requirement for the audience is to keep a running list of books that they might someday want to read.

Logistics and Accountability

Many teachers shy away from independent reading because they find holding students accountable for the reading unreliable and time-consuming. In my opinion, this avoidance misses the point. I want students to feel accountable to themselves as readers. Teenagers should be setting their own reading goals, whether it is so many minutes a night, so many pages a week, or so many books a month. If students cheat by resorting to SparkNotes or copying another student's reading log, I want them to recognize that they are cheating themselves. I detest playing the role of a warder, policing students' progress in a book. Instead, I try to help students make their own decisions about books, offering friendly and easily ignorable suggestions regarding next steps. For example:

- ◆ "Isn't that the fifth Rick Riordan book you've read this semester? How about trying something by Francesca Lia Block? I love her Weetzie Bat books, about growing up on the wild side of Los Angeles."

- ◆ "I see you've been reading *The Golden Compass* for a month now. Are you enjoying it? Want to put it down and try a different fantasy author? Have you tried Neal Gaiman's *Neverwhere*?"

- ◆ "Everything you've read lately has been fiction. Have you checked out the nonfiction shelves? I usually read fiction, too, but could not put down Phillip Hoose's *The Boys Who Challenged Hitler*. It tells the story of a group of teenage boys who inspired the resistance movement in Denmark. Take a look. See what you think."

I am much less interested in catching students who do not do what I expect than I am in promoting joyful reading among those who do. Point systems for keeping track of students' progress always seem to get in the way of joyful reading. Should I allot more points to a long, easy book or to a short, complex novel? Should students who read slowly be punished for the pace at which they turn the page? Do I give credit for rereading a book? No system I ever came up with felt entirely fair. Nor did any point system ever properly reward what I cared about most—that students should acquire the habit of reading.

Becoming obsessed with accountability can distract us from our goal. This was brought home to me when my son was in eleventh grade and enrolled in an American literature class with an excellent teacher. I know she was wonderful because I taught Ms. Berman when she was in tenth grade. One evening I stuck my head into James' room to find him randomly placing sticky notes throughout Upton Sinclair's *The Jungle*. "James! What are you doing?" I demanded.

"Ah, oh, yeah, Mom. I have a reading conference with Ms. Berman tomorrow, but I only read fifty pages. If she sees all the stickies, she'll think I finished the book. Don't worry. I can keep her talking on what I read."

This situation posed a dilemma for me. I really needed James to get an A in that class, get into college, and get out of the house, so I shook my head and shut the door. The story has an interesting ending, though. James did indeed keep his teacher talking, earn the A, and graduate from college. Fast-forward a few years, and he is working for a firm in downtown Chicago. Dinner-table conversation turns to the stockyards and without blinking an eye, James begins expounding on *The Jungle* and the evils of the old meatpacking industry, warning us of the hazards entailed in consuming hot dogs.

The moral of the story? Reading fifty pages of a book is better than reading no pages. Don't worry if students like James find ways to short-circuit your account-ability measures. Continue expecting students to read independently; it is the right thing to do. In *Reading in the Wild: The Book Whisperer's Keys to Cultivating Lifelong Reading Habits*, Donalyn Miller explains why:

> I want my students to enjoy reading and find it meaningful when they are in my class, but I also want them to understand why reading matters to their lives. A reading workshop classroom provides a temporary scaffold, but eventually students must have self-efficacy and the tools they need to go it alone. The goal of all reading instruction is independence. If students remain dependent on teachers to remove all obstacles that prevent them from reading, they won't become independent readers. (Miller with Kelly 2013, xviii)

Persuading students to read for you or for points or for a grade is not enough. We need to persuade them to read for themselves and not only because it might raise their ACT and SAT scores (which it will). Without books in their lives, the world will seem a much smaller, more confined space. With books, they have a passport to the planet. And as Emily Dickinson reminds us, "this Traverse may the poorest take/ without oppress of toll" (2013, 157).

In *The Reading Zone: How to Help Kids Become Skilled, Passionate, Habitual, Critical Readers*, Nancie Atwell and Ann Atwell Merkel (2016) describe how their seventh and eighth graders read an average of forty to fifty books a year. When kids navigate so many pages, it's hard to keep them from becoming competent and confident readers. Voluminous reading also helps young people evolve into competent and confident adults. Books teach them more than we, their teachers, ever could.

The Bad Habits of Good Readers

A chapter on helping students become avid readers would be incomplete without taking into consideration some of the bad habits of good readers. Too often, such readers (and I include myself here) do the following:

1. *Value speed over reflection.* They seldom pause between books to think about what they have read, reaching for the next one with hardly an intake of breath.

2. *Skip anything they find boring.* Unlike inexpert readers, these accomplished readers feel free to jump past anything that interrupts the flow of a story. They skim descriptive passages and ignore altogether embedded poetry or quotations.

3. *Care more about their personal reading than the assigned reading.* I have known many avid readers who have performed very poorly in high school, preferring to prop a book inside their textbook and simply read their way through the school day. I know because I was one of these students, at least in geometry class.

4. *Declare a text they do not care for as "boring" with great authority.* This can be disruptive because classmates who have hardly read a word of *A Tale of Two Cities* find support in their antipathy for Dickens from a student who did not enjoy the novel but nevertheless finished it over the weekend.

5. *Write poorly and spell carelessly.* In their desire to get back to their book, these readers often rush through writing assignments. Wide reading has given them knowledge of many things, and so avid readers are able to dash something off that passes muster, but they are reluctant to spend the kind of time revising that would actually make the quality of their writing match the quality of their thinking.

6. *Become mired in a genre, reading one particular kind of book for a very long time.* Lynne Sharon Schwartz writes in *Ruined by Reading*:

   > [I] read every novel by Jean Rhys and Barbara Pym as soon as I could get my hands on them. It was like eating candy—the chocolate-covered nuts of the cinema or the celebrated potato chips of which you can't eat just one. The variations in their novels were in fact no more than the slightly different planes and convolutions in each potato chip, and each one predictably tasty. I became an expert in self-indulgence. (2001, 103)

Teenagers can easily wallow in John Greene novels. Please don't think I am criticizing compelling narratives like *The Fault in Our Stars* and *Looking for Alaska*. What I am suggesting is that a teacher might want to nudge some John Greene fans toward a wider range of authors, settings, and genres. His books will always be there as comfort food.

While good readers are able to meet state reading standards and often achieve at the highest levels on standardized tests, I believe they can be helped to become more thoughtful readers.

> *While good readers are able to meet state reading standards and often achieve at the highest levels on standardized tests, I believe they can be helped to become more thoughtful readers.*

I recall my own first reading of Zora Neal Hurston's *Their Eyes Were Watching God*. As usual I had barreled through the novel at breakneck speed and went to my book-club meeting wondering what all the fuss was about. Fortunately I didn't make a fool of myself (as I might have done at sixteen years old) by declaring the book boring. Instead I kept my mouth shut and listened to what others had to say. It dawned on me as they spoke that in my race through the book, I had missed quite a lot. In fact, it seemed that I had missed it all. I needed to read Janie Crawford's story with greater care.

The best thing about being a competent, confident, and compulsive reader is that going back to reread a book isn't a problem. I don't exactly know how, but constant readers always seem to find time where others find none.

CHAPTER 4

Teaching with Intention and Heart

Our skill, our learning, and our commitment to the text will determine, for each of us, the kind of experience that the text provides. Learning to read books—or pictures, or films—is not merely an academic experience but a way of accepting the fact that our lives are of limited duration and that whatever satisfaction we may achieve in life must come through the strength of our engagement with what is around us.
—Robert Scholes, *Protocols of Reading*

Reading literature stimulates our imaginations. It transports us to ancient and future worlds impossible to explore outside the pages of a book. It exposes traits all mankind seems to share—the lust for power, the pursuit of love, the ache for experience—as well as the acute differences among peoples and cultures. As such, it is intellectually unsettling. That is a good thing.

I believe we err when we tell students, "Reading is fun!" though not because it cannot be. The mistake is equating reading literature with entertainment. Books like *1984* were designed to disturb, not amuse, readers. In his essay "Why I Write," George Orwell explains that he was motivated by a "desire to push the world in a certain direction, to alter other people's idea of the kind of society that they should strive after" (1946). To be sure, there is pleasure to be had from reading *1984* but not the same kind of pleasure one takes from an amusement park.

Students often wonder why the books they read for English class rarely have happy endings. *Romeo and Juliet* ends tragically. Anne Frank dies young. The jury decides against Atticus Finch. Aristotle used the term *catharsis* to describe how the pitiable and fearful incidents that occur in Greek tragedy arouse powerful emotions in the audience. Though we suffer with the protagonist through a series of unfortunate events, viewers emerge from the theatre satisfied. Despite the unhappy ending, the conflict has been resolved in a way that corresponds with the audience's experience of human nature and with the ironies of fate. A tragedy's outcome may not be the one we hoped for, but it nevertheless proceeds logically from the protagonist's actions.

Students sometimes do not see why they should have to feel the hero's pain. I try to explain that expressed within many seemingly heartbreaking narratives are themes of enduring love and the resilience of the human spirit. Literature teaches us how to survive.

In Richard Wright's autobiography, *Black Boy* (2007), the nine-year-old Richard is mugged coming home from the grocery store. His mother sends him back outside with a stick. She understands that the world is a brutal place, so instead of comforting her traumatized child, she forces him back out into the street to confront the trouble that surrounds him. Ultimately Richard finds his way onto and beyond those mean streets through reading and writing. *Black Boy* invites students to experience vicariously the debilitating effects of poverty and discrimination and to begin to understand why the struggle for economic justice and civil rights is everyone's business. Alongside history and philosophy, the study of literature offers a powerful means of understanding the problems that continue to beset humanity.

Unless English teachers intentionally make great books like *Black Boy* central to the curriculum, few students will choose to invest the time and effort to read them. Novels like Toni Morrison's *Beloved* or *Song of Solomon* are challenging not just for teenage readers but for all readers. Morrison—along with Dickens, Hardy, the Brontë sisters, Twain, Hemingway, Fitzgerald, Flaubert, Dostoyevsky, Fuentes, García Márquez, Mahfouz, and Gordimer—has complex things to say that cannot be captured in a simple, straightforward narrative or in simple language.

In many ways, these books are too difficult for students to read on their own. But there is a gulf between what students can read alone and what they are able to read with the help of a teacher. Merely to assign and then to assess students' comprehension of challenging literature in the name of rigor is a recipe for failure. It also makes students hate reading. Wouldn't you hate to read if you had to answer a set of questions at the conclusion of every chapter? Would you not be tempted to copy from your friend's paper? Along with choosing great books to teach, we need to teach in ways that don't feel like torture. Acknowledge to students that reading *Wuthering Heights* may occasionally be difficult, and in the very next breath, assure them that your job is to help them over the hurdles.

Every winter break I set myself the challenge of picking up a classic that I've never read before. Last Christmas I chose William Faulkner's *Absalom, Absalom!* (1990a). Having taught *The Sound and the Fury* (1990b), I was familiar with Faulkner's Yoknapatawpha County, but fifteen pages into *Absalom, Absalom!* I ground to a halt. My eyes were reading the words, but I had no feeling for where the story was going or who was saying what to whom. What to do? I reached for my laptop and proceeded to Wikipedia. The plot summary and list of characters gave me just enough of a nudge forward to make the novel accessible. I tell this story about myself—a mature and experienced reader—because it is easy to forget just how difficult some books can be to navigate and how a little help at the right moment can make all the difference.

Making Intentional Choices About Which Books to Teach

In *The Anatomy of Influence: Literature as a Way of Life*, Harold Bloom (2011) proposes three criteria for choosing works to be read and reread and taught to others: aesthetic splendor, cognitive power, and wisdom. The books we intend for the whole class to read must be beautifully, masterfully written. Their language should be worthy of close examination and inspire awe in the reader. A perfect example is this arresting passage from the first page of Joseph Conrad's *Heart of Darkness*:

The sea-reach of the Thames stretched before us like the beginning
of an interminable waterway. In the offing the sea and the sky
were welded together without a joint, and in the luminous space
the tanned sails of the barges drifting up with the tide seemed to
stand still in red clusters of canvas sharply peaked, with gleams of
varnished sprits. A haze rested on the low shores that ran out to sea
in vanishing flatness. (2006 Project Gutenberg)

Cognitively powerful books teach students by describing places, people, and
events that would be otherwise outside students' ken. They also have the power to
suggest important ideas to readers, but the ideas must flow from a wise source.
The books we teach should offer readers insight into what it means to be human.
Shakespeare's plays are in my opinion the finest examples of aesthetically splendid,
cognitively powerful, and wise texts in English, but many other voices sing as sweetly.

That said, teachers are going to have to do more than simply hand out copies of
Romeo and Juliet and expect ninth graders to be enthralled by its aesthetic splendor.
Making complex works accessible to young readers, particularly readers whose reading
and language skills lag behind their thinking skills, requires artful and intentional
instruction. One way to introduce Sophocles' *Antigone* might be to have students
write about a time when they stood up to authority, preparing them for the argument
between Antigone and her uncle Creon, the king of Thebes. A much less effective
intro activity would be to prepare students for *Macbeth* and Lady Macbeth's "Out,
damned spot! Out, I say" speech by asking them to turn and talk with a partner about
a time when they had a stubborn spot on their hands. Tapping prior experience must
prepare students for the important issues they will encounter in the text.

English teachers have invested a great deal of effort in an attempt to make
literature study easier and more relevant to students' lives. The hope was that if
students didn't have to struggle to read text, they might be more engaged in their
learning and more amenable to reading. The result in terms of the books being
taught was a loss of rigor. That need not have been the case. Works by contemporary
novelists like Colson Whitehead, Viet Thanh Nguyen, and Jhumpa Lahiri focus on
relevant issues and possess all the cognitive power and aesthetic splendor of Jane
Austen, Mark Twain, and Mary Shelley. But because these contemporary complex
texts pose the very same textual challenges as classic works (difficult vocabulary,
complicated syntax, figurative language, and hefty page counts), we too often choose
to teach simpler books.

I have bought many class sets of shorter, easier, funnier books that I thought would appeal to teenagers. But teaching such titles didn't solve the problem of engagement. My avid readers finished the books overnight, and the struggling readers still complained that they were boring and refused to read. I was most dissatisfied with the quality of conversation. Simpler books failed to inspire discussion about important issues and big ideas. They didn't pose troubling questions or challenge readers to reconsider what they thought they believed. There was nothing to talk about. I was reminded of adult book-club meetings I have attended where we've all said we enjoyed the book—for example, Robert Harris' *Conclave*—but after fifteen minutes have run out of things to say and started talking about our kids. That's not what I join a book club for, and it is not what I want for my students.

Instead of searching for works that pose few challenges for young readers, we need to design lessons that provide access to complex texts.

What It Means to Teach a Book

Too often the teaching of literature has been an occasion for teachers who know and love books to showcase what they love and show off what they know. Students come away from such classes—and this is when they are done well—in awe of their teachers but with little confidence in their own ability to read literature. As Louise Rosenblatt explained, "the problem that a teacher faces first of all, then, is the creation of a situation favorable to a vital experience of literature. Unfortunately, many of the practices and much of the tone of literature teaching have precisely the opposite effect" (1983, 61).

Without intending to, English teachers beat books to death. Refusing to let go until we've explained every allusion and unpacked every metaphor, we take six, eight, even ten weeks to teach a novel. Well before we've turned the last page, all parties—both students and teacher—are bored to tears. Most novels can and should be taught in a concentrated four weeks.

Before you assume that I've lost my mind and have no concept of how much reading teenagers will and won't do each evening, let me explain. I believe it is a mistake to parse out reading assignments by dividing the book into equal chunks. This isn't how one naturally reads. A novel has momentum. While the opening chapters may require slow and careful reading with judicious instruction at every step to help students identify the main characters, establish the setting, and become familiar with the author's style, readers can and should move more quickly through subsequent chapters.

This doesn't mean that the teacher's work is done once the class has navigated the opening chapters of a novel. Essential passages, for example, the first three paragraphs of Chapter 5 in Mary Shelley's *Frankenstein* (Project Gutenberg 2008), where the monster comes alive, deserve careful scrutiny. I take an entire period to reread and discuss the text sentence by sentence, image by image. If students skimmed over this page without comprehending what occurred, the rest of the novel would make little sense. My job is to identify such passages and, in Louise Rosenblatt's words, create "a situation favorable to a vital experience of literature." Let me describe what this kind of intentional instruction would look like in my classroom. First, the paragraphs from Chapter 5:

> It was on a dreary night of November, that I beheld the accomplishment of my toils. With an anxiety that almost amounted to agony, I collected the instruments of life around me, that I might infuse a spark of being into the lifeless thing that lay at my feet. It was already one in the morning; the rain pattered dismally against the panes, and my candle was nearly burnt out, when, by the glimmer of the half-extinguished light, I saw the dull yellow eye of the creature open; it breathed hard, and a convulsive motion agitated its limbs.
>
> How can I describe my emotions at this catastrophe, or how delineate the wretch whom with such infinite pains and care I had endeavoured to form? His limbs were in proportion, and I had selected his features as beautiful. Beautiful!—Great God! His yellow skin scarcely covered the work of muscles and arteries beneath; his hair was of a lustrous black, and flowing; his teeth of a pearly whiteness; but these luxuriances only formed a more horrid contrast with his watery eyes, that seemed almost of the same colour as the dun white sockets in which they were set, his shrivelled complexion and straight black lips.
>
> The different accidents of life are not so changeable as the feelings of human nature. I had worked hard for nearly two years, for the sole purpose of infusing life into an inanimate body. For this I had deprived myself of rest and health. I had desired it with an ardour that far exceeded moderation; but now that I had finished, the beauty of the dream vanished, and breathless horror and

disgust filled my heart. Unable to endure the aspect of the being I had created, I rushed out of the room, and continued a long time traversing my bedchamber, unable to compose my mind to sleep. At length lassitude succeeded to the tumult I had before endured; and I threw myself on the bed in my clothes, endeavouring to seek a few moments of forgetfulness. But it was in vain: I slept, indeed, but I was disturbed by the wildest dreams. I thought I saw Elizabeth, in the bloom of health, walking in the streets of Ingolstadt. Delighted and surprised, I embraced her; but as I imprinted the first kiss on her lips, they became livid with the hue of death; her features appeared to change, and I thought that I held the corpse of my dead mother in my arms; a shroud enveloped her form, and I saw the grave-worms crawling in the folds of the flannel. I started from my sleep with horror; a cold dew covered my forehead, my teeth chattered, and every limb became convulsed: when, by the dim and yellow light of the moon, as it forced its way through the window shutters, I beheld the wretch—the miserable monster whom I had created. He held up the curtain of the bed; and his eyes, if eyes they may be called, were fixed on me. His jaws opened, and he muttered some inarticulate sounds, while a grin wrinkled his cheeks. He might have spoken, but I did not hear; one hand was stretched out, seemingly to detain me, but I escaped, and rushed downstairs. I took refuge in the courtyard belonging to the house which I inhabited; where I remained during the rest of the night, walking up and down in the greatest agitation, listening attentively, catching and fearing each sound as if it were to announce the approach of the demoniacal corpse to which I had so miserably given life. (Project Gutenberg 2008)

Although I assigned Chapter 5 for students to read for homework the night before, I begin class by handing out copies of the first three paragraphs on a sheet of paper they can annotate and ask them to reread the first three paragraphs, noting words and phrases that contribute to the passage's mood.

By design, I do not start class with a quiz. Rather than waste instructional time catching students who have not done the reading or falsely rewarding those who resorted to SparkNotes, I choose to invest the time reading this critical passage purposefully. My goal for the lesson is to ensure that every student leaves with a clear understanding of what Mary Shelley is describing and what Victor Frankenstein is thinking and feeling.

When I see that everyone has finished reading the passage, I ask five students to copy onto the board one of the lines they marked. Teenagers need good reasons to stand up and move. It helps keep them engaged in the work. With Mary Shelley's evocative language displayed in front of us, I tell students to turn to a partner and explain in their own words what happened in the first paragraph. If neither of the students is sure, I suggest that they ask another pair of readers for help. It's important for students not to see me, their teacher, as the only source of information.

> *Teenagers need good reasons to stand up and move. It helps keep them engaged in the work.*

I then ask for volunteers to read aloud the first paragraph as dramatically as they can, taking advantage of the stage directions the text offers. Inevitably other students want to offer their interpretations of Victor Frankenstein's actions. We listen to a few before moving on to paragraph two.

In the second paragraph, the scientist describes his immediate reactions to the creature he created. Together we discuss these questions:

- How would you describe Victor Frankenstein's reaction?
- What do his choice of words (calling it a wretch, for example) suggest about Victor's response to his creation?
- What do you think went wrong?

The third paragraph poses the greatest textual challenges, so we pause to write before we talk. I ask students to describe Victor Frankenstein's dream and explain what they think the dream suggests about his state of mind. When I see that students are no longer writing, I quickly assemble them into small groups and ask them to use what they have written to talk about the implications of Victor's dream.

As the class period draws to a close, we talk about this passage: "His jaws opened, and he muttered some inarticulate sounds, while a grin wrinkled his cheeks. He might have spoken, but I did not hear; one hand was stretched out, seemingly to detain me, but I escaped, and rushed down stairs." I ask:

- What might "the monster" (Victor's word) have wanted to say to Victor?
- What do you think his grin suggests?
- How do you think he might have felt when Victor ran from the room?

Not every page of *Frankenstein* is worthy of this kind of close reading. When teachers require students to treat every one as though it were—annotating every page or answering detailed questions at the conclusion of every chapter—we wring the pleasure out of reading.

What About Students Who Are Still Learning English?

According to the National Center for Education Statistics (2018), 4.6 million public school students are English language learners, 14.1 percent of total public school enrollment. In the last decade, thirty states have seen an increase in the number of English learners, with the largest increase (.6 of a percentage point) in Kansas. In California, English learners make up 22.4 percent of the student population. Spanish was the home language of 3.7 million ELL students in 2014–15, representing 77.1 percent of all ELL students and 7.6 percent of all public K–12 students. Arabic, Chinese, and Vietnamese were the next most common home languages.

Because adolescent English learners are developing their English and learning content at the same time, the challenge they face in school is greatly more demanding than that of native speakers. While some students are able to rise to this challenge, others are overwhelmed. In a report to the Carnegie Foundation called *Double the Work* (Short and Fitzsimmons 2007), researchers describe the many differences among English learners, differences the label of ELL often masks.

English learners who enter American schools as adolescents possess varying levels of language proficiency in their native language as well as in English. Some speak a combination of English and their native language with varying degrees of grammatical accuracy. These students also have enormous differences in their knowledge of academic subject matter. Many first-generation immigrants have had their education disrupted in their home or as they traveled to America. Sometimes schools will place older students in lower grades than others of their age because they cannot demonstrate proof of prior academic course work.

It may surprise you to learn that 57 percent of adolescent English learners were born in the United States and have attended American schools since kindergarten or first grade. Many of these students have limited English proficiency, which suggests that our schools have let these students down. Of the 43 percent who are foreign-born, those who enter American schools in middle and high school are often more challenged than those entering at an earlier age largely because learning a language later in life is more difficult. These students have fewer years to master English as well as the rest of a demanding high school curriculum (Short and Fitzsimmons, 2007).

Immigrant families often need their children to help with childcare and part-time jobs for financial reasons. Some of these teenagers are undocumented, a factor that affects both their socioeconomic status and, in some states, their postsecondary educational options. There is also a wide variation among adolescent English learners in terms of their commitment to school, their parents' educational levels and proficiency in English, and many other factors that influence their literacy development.

It is vital that teachers be responsive to and responsible for helping all middle and high school–age English learners, whatever their background. These young people are here to stay. We need all students not just to survive but to thrive in school and develop confidence in their ability to continue their education. It is vital to the future of this country.

Lily Wong Fillmore (in Zehr 2010), a longtime researcher into English language learning, has made an impassioned plea to teachers not to dumb down texts for English learners. Worried about the "gradual erosion of the complexity of texts" offered to students, Fillmore posits that when teachers offer only simplified materials to their English learners, it is "niceness run amok." While she acknowledges that for the first years English learners need altered or alternate texts, ultimately they deserve the challenge of rich literature.

In order to help make complex texts accessible to English learners, have students calculate how much time it will take to complete the assigned reading. When you are past the first few chapters of a book and ready to cover more pages overnight, have students time themselves as they read for fifteen minutes. Then

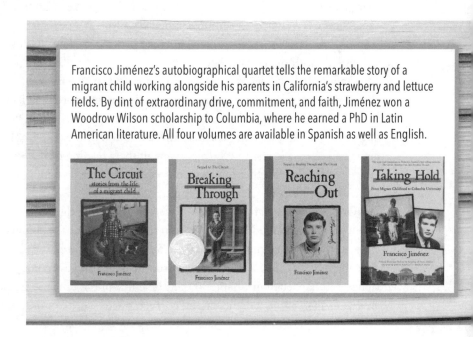

Francisco Jiménez's autobiographical quartet tells the remarkable story of a migrant child working alongside his parents in California's strawberry and lettuce fields. By dint of extraordinary drive, commitment, and faith, Jiménez won a Woodrow Wilson scholarship to Columbia, where he earned a PhD in Latin American literature. All four volumes are available in Spanish as well as English.

ask them to note how many pages they were able to read in the quarter of an hour. Multiply that number by four. This will give students the number of pages they are able to read in an hour. Divide that number by sixty, and students will have the number of pages they read per minute. For most English learners, it will be a figure less than one. This information helps students figure out how long the thirty-page reading assignment will take them to complete. The exercise helps clarify what doing "double the work" really means.

E-readers allow English learners easy access to the definitions of unfamiliar words. Unfortunately, the definitions are in English. Students need the English word translated at a touch to their home language. Software engineers must surely be developing applications to make this possible, but I haven't yet found one that works faultlessly. Having a bilingual dictionary at hand, in print or online, still seems the best solution.

Audio recordings of a novel can also assist English learners, particularly if students read along in the text as they listen. Dialogue is almost always easier to comprehend when read with expression. As with many aids, audio recordings should supplement, not supplant, the reading.

For students who are biliterate, where available, provide them with bilingual editions of the book the class is reading or a copy of the work in their home language. If the class is reading an English translation, for example of Gabriel García Márquez's *Chronicle of a Death Foretold*, the Spanish speakers can become resident experts on word choice, explaining to their English-only peers what was lost in translation. When teaching poetry, I always try to provide students with the original poem side by side with the translation.

Online study guides, if employed judiciously, can also keep students from abandoning a book. A great work of literature is much more than its plot summary. Folger Library editions of Shakespeare's plays offer readers thumbnail sketches of every scene, and we don't consider this a dilution of the text. English learners benefit from easy access to such a preview of their reading of *Lord of the Flies* or *The Catcher in the Rye*, whether that preview comes from you as a kind of trailer for the homework reading or from SparkNotes.

One way to check that students are actually reading the book and not relying solely on the study guide is to copy from the online guide the summary of the chapter you have assigned, say, Chapter 6 of *The Great Gatsby*. At the beginning of class the next day, display the summary on the board and ask students to write four things that happened in Chapter 6 that the guide doesn't mention. Along with being an easy assessment to administer and correct, the quiz sends students the message that you know about these guides and are keen that they should not abuse them. I often say to students, "You wouldn't want anyone else chewing your food for you, would you? Then why let someone else read a book for you?"

Most importantly, we need to provide English learners with daily opportunities to talk with peers about what they are reading and thinking. It is essential for these students to participate in class discussions and develop confidence in their ability to analyze literature even as they are acquiring the language. To help them become more adept at speaking in a formal register, model and have students practice composing their thoughts using academic language. Sentence starters can help:

- While I understand what you just said, in my opinion . . .
- As I read the chapter I noticed that again and again . . .
- Can you offer more evidence for that? To my mind . . .
- The part of the story that completely baffled me was . . .
- I read that differently. Why do you think . . .
- When I read that passage I thought . . .
- On the one hand . . . , while on the other . . .
- The quotation that made me doubt what you say . . .
- I concede that . . . but still feel . . .

A common misuse of such templates occurs when teachers hand students a list of sentence starters and ask them to fill in the blanks. Not only does this approach lend itself to easy cheating, but such worksheets miss the point. It is the language of the template that we need students to appropriate. Though it may at first seem artificial to have students employ these sentence starters in conversation, with practice, the more formal constructions begin to feel comfortable in their mouths. Eavesdropping on students as they talk in small groups, I find that sophisticated sentence structures seem to stimulate more nuanced thinking. It may have struck you that these approaches to working with English learners would be of help to any student. You would be correct.

When we relegate students to books that match their language skills but fall far below the level of their intellectual interests, school becomes increasingly meaningless. Literature has the power to stimulate thought, ranging over moral, philosophical, and ontological issues that have challenged humans through the ages. With intentional teaching and a commitment to the task, it is possible to unleash this power in our classrooms.

CHAPTER 5

Words, Words, Words

In homes where the near friends and visitors are mainly literary people—lawyers, judges, professors and clergymen—the children's ears become early familiarized with wide vocabularies. It is natural for them to pick up any words that fall their way; it is natural for them to pick up big and little ones indiscriminately; it is natural for them to use without fear any word that comes to their net, no matter how formidable it may be as to size.

—Mark Twain, *Autobiography*

Teachers devote large swathes of classroom time to vocabulary instruction: defining words, drawing pictures of words, playing word games, reviewing words, quizzing students on words. I know why I liked teaching vocabulary this way. The quizzes gave me twenty minutes of welcome peace while students took them; the tests were easy to grade and slotted tidily into my electronic grade book. Parents were delighted to see their children studying lists of words. It felt like school. While focusing on vocabulary is ostensibly in accord with the push for college readiness, I began to be concerned that my students were spending too much time with vocabulary activities and too little time learning new words.

I was also troubled by my students' quiz results. Typical A students who studied the list received their As. No surprise there. But it was also the case that students who were native English speakers and already knew most of the words on the list often earned Bs without doing a lick of work. What bothered me most were my English language learners, who sweated to learn ten out of the twenty words and still failed the quiz. Something didn't seem right. Rather than rewarding students for learning ten new words, the system I had created made it hard for them ever to earn a good grade in the class. It was rigged.

I knew I needed to do more than revise my grading practices; I needed to rethink the principles underpinning how I taught vocabulary. And the more I thought about it, the more it seemed to me that a list-based approach was a waste of time. Before declaring me a heretic, consider this: most of the words that you know weren't learned from any vocabulary list or program but from reading.

Meet Words in Context

Students with robust vocabularies understand more of what they read, creating a "Matthew effect," whereby those who already *have* get more (Stanovich 1986). Since comprehension comes more easily for students who know more words, they tend to read more. The more they read, the more competent they become at figuring out unfamiliar words. While such students may be unable to define *cantankerous*, they would not be thrown for a loop by a passage such as the following:

> In the restaurant Maggie's aunt grumbled about everything—
> the food, the service, the price. She was the most cantankerous
> company imaginable.

The text surrounding *cantankerous* helps readers understand the word. Clearly a single exposure is never enough, as no one particular context is likely to embody a word's full meaning. The practice of meeting words in context is a more authentic approach to learning vocabulary than memorizing dictionary definitions (Adams 2010–11). In my experience, even those students who correctly match *cantankerous* to *contentious* on Friday's quiz are unlikely to remember its meaning for long or to use the word in their speech or writing until they meet it several more times in the course of their reading.

In order to establish a new word in long-term memory, students need to encounter the word in several different contexts. With frequent exposures—which occur only when students read broadly and often—students develop a full sense of a word's meaning. I also want students to grasp the nuances that distinguish *cantankerous* from *contentious* or *peevish*. While *cantankerous* suggests bad temper and the refusal to cooperate, *contentious* carries a more argumentative and controversial connotation. *Peevishness*, on the other hand, conjures up the image of irritability particularly over unimportant things. Words may have similar meanings, but their connotations are rarely identical. If they were, we wouldn't need two distinct words.

Teachers can help students develop the habit of learning new words by drawing attention to words in the course of a lesson, modeling the kind of thinking a good reader employs when meeting an unfamiliar word. Ideally, this habit of mind should be fostered even before children can read for themselves. For example, Beatrix Potter (2012) uses the word *soporific* in "The Tale of the Flopsy Bunnies" multiple times along with clues to the word's meaning.

It is said that the effect of eating too much lettuce is "soporific."

I have never felt sleepy after eating lettuces; but then I am not a rabbit.

They certainly had a very soporific effect upon the Flopsy Bunnies!

If you asked most ninth graders what *soporific* means, they wouldn't have a clue, yet generations of small children have had no trouble following the action in "The Tale of the Flopsy Bunnies." How is this possible? I believe we underestimate how stories themselves offer clues to the meaning of words. Along with her charming illustration of snoozing bunnies, Beatrix Potter goes on to explain, "By degrees, one after another, they were overcome with slumber and lay down in the mown grass." The author offers all the clues a reader needs for understanding the meaning of *soporific*. Later in the tale the word appears again:

The little rabbits smiled sweetly in their sleep under the shower of grass; they did not awake because the lettuce had been so soporific.

Engaged in the story, children absorb new words and their meanings. Other vocabulary that you might be surprised to find in this work of classic and enduring children's literature includes *doleful*, *profusely*, *resourceful*, and *improvident*. Rather than teaching long lists of words in an attempt to inoculate students against ever meeting a word they don't know, we need to expose students to literature that employs gorgeous language and ask questions that point to clues in the context.

Explicit Vocabulary Instruction

Building students' vocabulary implicitly through the close reading of complex texts does not obviate the need for explicit instruction. Students who apply their knowledge of Greek and Latin roots and familiarity with affixes possess powerful tools for figuring out an unfamiliar word's meaning. I am often deeply annoyed by my inability to find a word my husband doesn't know. Again and again I have watched him reach back in his memory to the Latin he learned from the age of seven and the Greek he learned from nine.

That said, requiring students to memorize long lists of roots and their definitions alone is unlikely to foster a love of word learning. I despair when I see comprehensive lists of prefixes and suffixes incorporated into instructional worksheets. Did you know that the four most frequently used prefixes account for 97 percent of prefixed words in printed school English (Honig et al. 2000)?

- ◆ dis-, de-
- ◆ in-, im-, il-, ir-
- ◆ re-
- ◆ un-

> *. . . requiring students to memorize long lists of roots and their definitions alone is unlikely to foster a love of word learning.*

We need to model for students how adept readers figure out the meanings of unfamiliar words using every clue at their disposal for unlocking the meaning of words.

Let's take, for example, the word *inaudible*. Most students would know that *audio* is related to the reception or reproduction of sound. You might take a moment to contrast *audio* with *video*. The prefix *in*—like *im* (*improbable*, *immeasurable*),

ir- (*irregular, irresponsible*), and *un-* (*unlikely, unintentional*)—indicates the word's converse is the case (*inexpensive, indescribable, indefensible*). The suffix *-ible* ("able to be") wraps up the word, so a working definition of *inaudible* is "not audible, or incapable of being heard." Ideally you want to make every unpacking of a word an opportunity for demonstrating the relationships among words.

> *. . . certain words, often nouns, sometimes need to be taught in order for students to make sense of the text*

Given the enormous number of words in the English language—the *Oxford English Dictionary* contains full entries for 171,476 words in current use—teachers need to choose carefully which words to teach (Beck, McKeown, and Kucan 2002). Trying to preteach every word a child might not know before reading can take up more instructional time than the reading itself. That said, certain words, often nouns, sometimes need to be taught in order for students to make sense of the text. The first paragraph of Kenneth Grahame's *The Wind in the Willows* offers an example.

The passage contains several words a child might not know (and one made-up word), but context, illustrations, and a modicum of guesswork will yield almost complete comprehension. Indeed, for the typical urban child, the word *mole* might be the most unfamiliar.

> The Mole had been working very hard all the morning, spring-cleaning his little home. First with brooms, then with dusters; then on ladders and steps and chairs, with a brush and a pail of whitewash; till he had dust in his throat and eyes, and splashes of whitewash all over his black fur, and an aching back and weary arms. Spring was moving in the air above and in the earth below and around him, penetrating even his dark and lowly little house with its spirit of divine discontent and longing. It was small wonder, then, that he suddenly flung down his brush on the floor, said, "Bother!" and "O blow!" and also "Hang spring-cleaning!" and bolted out of the house without even waiting to put on his coat. Something up above was calling him imperiously, and he made for the steep little tunnel which answered in his case to the gravelled carriage-drive owned by animals whose residences are nearer to the sun and air. So he scraped and scratched and scrabbled and scrooged, and then he scrooged again and scrabbled and scratched and scraped, working busily with his little paws and muttering to himself, "Up we go! Up we go!" till at last, pop! his snout came out

into the sunlight and he found himself rolling in the warm grass of
a great meadow. (1908, 1–2)

While students might not be familiar with the word *whitewash*, you could
invite them to notice how Mole was standing on a ladder with a brush and pail of
whitewash to spring-clean his house. Directing their attention to these context clues
along with pointing out the two parts of the word—*white* and *wash*—are probably
all you need to do to establish a picture of what is going on here. This kind of word
study models for young readers what good readers do instinctively.

Words with multiple meanings can be particularly challenging for English
learners. While students may be familiar with the noun *bolt* and the idea of *bolting
a door shut*, the intransitive use of the verb *bolted*, meaning to make a sudden, swift
dash, might be puzzling. When you notice such usage, try to make a point of drawing
students' attention to it in the course of the lesson. Ask students to share examples
of times when they bolted from a room. Learning about words is a lifelong project.
Celebrate that you have discovered an additional use for a known word.

Not to play with Kenneth Grahame's artful use of the sound of words borders on
educational malpractice.

So he scraped and scratched and scrabbled and scrooged, and
then he scrooged again and scrabbled and scratched and scraped,
working busily with his little paws. . . .

Ask students what effect this description of Mole's actions with his paws had on
their understanding of where he lived. Take a moment to act out what this might look
like. Reflect on the order of the repeated words. Why all the alliteration, and what in
the world does *scrooged* mean anyway? Grahame is playing with words. Play along.

The Specific Gravity of Words

Blithely skipping words you don't know is a recipe for reading comprehension disaster,
unless you can be certain that the unfamiliar words are relatively unimportant to the
text's overall meaning. For example, in a description of a bucolic woodland glade where

the author regales you with a list of wildflowers, you might choose to gloss over the meaning of *agrimony*, *baneberry*, and *gilly-weed*, as the overall picture is clear. Though such word choices are intentional on the part of the writer and nuance will be lost, stopping to look up such words causes readers to lose momentum and possibly the thread without adding much to their comprehension of the whole.

Of course everything depends upon the reader's purpose. If I pick up a book in order to identify the wildflowers in my garden, I am going to pay very careful attention to the names of individual specimens. Good readers have a sense of when a word is cardinal to understanding a passage and when it is not. I must confess that though I love Patrick O'Brian's *Master and Commander* series, I cannot be bothered to learn the vocabulary of nineteenth-century sailing ships. Every book contains a helpful diagram with parts clearly labeled: spanker, boom, mizzen mast, futtock shrouds. I ignore the drawing and read right through every term, keeping my eye instead on the story of Captain Jack Aubry and his friend, the ship's surgeon and spy, Stephen Maturin. The purpose of my reading is pleasure, not the acquisition of nautical details.

I had a similar experience recently while reading Tim Winton's *Island Home*, a landscape memoir of growing up and living in Australia. The book is a love song to the land. Early in the text Winton describes his childhood backyard that backed onto bush and wetlands.

> On one side of the jarrah picket fences, parched buffalo lawns and Hills Hoists. And on the other, a wilder world of frog-song and waterbirds where kids like us ran feral. We hunted for tadpoles, gilgies, bobtails and King's skinks and did what we could to knock writhing knots of spitfires from the limbs of tuarts and marri trees. Gilgies were a prize, but of all the treasures you could come home with, the greatest trophy was the long-necked turtle. (2017, 35)

If I had employed the five-finger rule some children are taught—where as soon as I met five words I didn't know, I must put the book down as too hard for me—I would have had to stop right there and then. But how much did it matter that I didn't recognize *jarrah* as the most common eucalyptus tree in Western Australia or that I had no idea *gilgies* are small freshwater crayfish? My mental picture of Winton's childhood pastimes may have lacked specifics, but the outline was clear. If I wanted to know more (and I did), I could easily pull up not only the definitions but also images of jarrah picket fences and gilgies with a few taps on my cell phone.

Instructional materials that simplify an author's original word choices in order to lower the reading level often reduce a text to its boring bare bones. Visualizing a young Tim Winton knocking "writhing knots of spitfires from the limbs of tuarts and marri trees" has a magical quality that I believe he fully intends his readers, whether native or foreign to Australia, to feel. He is painting a picture of Western Australia as a particular, treasured place that is in danger of being lost. He chose those words for a reason.

When J. K. Rowling was preparing the American version of her Harry Potter books, she consciously did not alter the vocabulary for her readers across the Atlantic. *Sweets* was not changed to *candy*, nor was *bloke* changed to *guy*. Millions of American readers figured out as they read that *to nick* meant "to steal" and what was intended when you called someone a *prat*. One change Rowling did make was to substitute *jacket* or *sweater* for *jumper*. Her reasoning was that *jumper* isn't so much an unfamiliar word but rather a word that describes very different pieces of clothing in Britain and the United States.

Do you know any readers who needed a glossary or who longed for a vocabulary lesson while reading *Harry Potter and the Philosopher's Stone*? Rowling trusted her readers, and millions of children have risen to the challenge. (*Guinness World Records 2018* estimates the series has sold over five hundred million copies around the world.)

But What About Tests?

If instruction and assessment focus only on rarely used multisyllabic words, we are going to frustrate students. Instead of fostering the love of word learning, we make kids feel dumb. Recognizing the limitations of list-based memorization, standardized tests have begun replacing traditional vocabulary items with ones that ask students to demonstrate their understanding of words in context. Test takers are now being asked to read a passage and answer questions designed to measure their understanding of what they have read. Along with these comprehension items, students are then pointed to a sentence within the passage and asked the meaning of a word in that particular context. All of the choices offered are correct definitions of the word, but only one of the choices is the correct answer in this context.

The good news is that students should no longer feel they need to cram for exams by memorizing lists of words they have never heard and are unlikely to meet anytime soon again. When was the last time you came across words like *uxorious*, *chimera*, or *limpid* in conversation or in print? Instead, invite students to explore the multiple meanings and shades of meaning suggested by the vocabulary in the texts you are reading and scrutinizing together. Point out to students how familiar nouns like *channel* or *prune* can have very different meanings when used as verbs. Consider the several meanings of *reservation* or *solution*. While native speakers can mostly navigate these vocabulary vagaries with ease, English learners often become frustrated. I don't blame them.

In order to perform well on high-stakes measures of vocabulary, students will have to know multiple meanings of a word, the kind of deep vocabulary knowledge that comes only with wide reading. We can no longer justify devoting weeks of instructional time to teaching the "Princeton hot 100 words" in order to help students be admitted to college. Forget the flashcards. Curb the quizzes. Instead, inspire students to read widely and wildly.

Having students look up words in a dictionary, copy out definitions, and use the words in meaning-laden sentences is an instructional practice that needs to be retired. Students will copy the shortest definition every time, no matter how archaic that particular usage, and most of their meaning-laden sentences employ the new words incorrectly. Such peripheral practices eat up precious classroom time and inadvertently suggest to students that learning words is disassociated from reading.

Possessing a broad vocabulary is important for much more than doing well on tests. The limits of students' language can define the borders of their thinking. A paucity of language can hamstring their ability to express themselves both in speaking and in writing. Word study should have a place of prominence in every lesson every day.

CHAPTER 6

Instructional Moves
That Matter

*We have overcomplicated instruction in reading, speaking,
and writing. To succeed, students simply need vastly more time to
purposefully read, discuss, and write about worthy,
substantive literature.*

—Michael Schmoker

Have you ever wondered how every sixteen-year-old, no matter how many grade
levels behind in reading, manages to read, understand, and pass a lengthy
multiple-choice test on the rules of the road? The combination of first-hand
experience as a passenger and the passionate desire to acquire a driver's license
creates the ideal conditions for reading comprehension. Even teenagers who have
fake-read their way through middle and high school rise to the challenge of this
not particularly well written, information-laden text. Why? They want to drive.

Consider the textual challenges the State of Illinois' *Rules of the Road* manual (2017) poses for young readers.

New Laws for 2017

- A bicyclist has all the rights and responsibilities applicable to a vehicle driver, including the right of way on roads and at intersections.

- A driver approaching a disabled vehicle using hazard lights on a four-lane roadway must move to the lane away from the disabled vehicle if safe to do so. If changing lanes is not possible, the driver must reduce speed when passing the disabled vehicle.

- A person commits vehicular endangerment when he/she causes an object to fall from an overpass or other elevated location in the direction of a moving vehicle with the intent to strike it.

- Vehicles are required to stop before meeting or overtaking a school bus located on school property (rather than just on public roadways).

I am particularly struck by the syntactical difficulty of the third bullet point. One has to visualize the scenario to understand the new law. *Vehicular endangerment* isn't exactly common usage, either. Yet teenagers navigate these abstrusely constructed sentences well enough to apply what they have learned on an exam. Most students can and do read well when they want to. If only we could package this motivation and apply it to the texts we need them to read in school.

Circumstances influence all of us as readers. Anyone who has had a loved one diagnosed with a medical problem and turned to the Internet for more information has had the experience of reading with limited background knowledge. Unfamiliar terminology confronts us on every line. We read, reread, look up definitions of words, scrutinize illustrations, and search out multiple sources because we have an urgent need to know.

As you read this page, you recognize letters of the alphabet, assemble the letters into words, and parse the words to make the sentences make sense. You bring to the text background knowledge from your experiences as a student and as a teacher. You understand educational terminology like *curriculum* and *assessment* and fill in the details of sketched classroom scenarios. You chose this book for a reason, most likely because you are a teacher and interested in improving your craft. You might have checked out my biography before beginning to read to see what credentials I bring to the table. You might be reading, pen in hand, agreeing or disagreeing with my argument, carrying on a conversation with the text as you read. These behaviors are second nature to you.

For many students, reading in school begins and ends with the first sentence of my previous paragraph. The vast majority are able to turn marks on a page into meaningful sentences but because they have little stake in the task and often no choice over what they are being asked to read, they invest almost nothing of themselves in the act of reading. Comprehension demands more of the reader.

Move 1: Push Students to Take Interpretive Risks

Unfortunately, students often give up as soon as they meet a textual road bump, deciding in an instant that the text is too hard for them. That is not necessarily the case. Books often contain rough patches and confusing passages. As I have already noted, able readers have the confidence to proceed with incomplete understanding, trusting that all will become clear in the end. Confident readers know to pause when something is unclear to ask themselves, "Did I ascribe an action to the wrong character? Was there a word I misread? Wait; could this be a flashback?"

Experienced readers instinctively speculate as they read. "Why did Catherine feel as she did about Heathcliff? Why is it always raining and stormy in this story? What might Catherine's and Heathcliff's hair colors and complexions suggest about their temperaments?" Such questions appear all too often on homework assignments and reading quizzes but actually belong inside readers' heads. Such speculation prods one to think more deeply as one reads. Nobody wants to stop reading to answer (in complete sentences, please) this kind of question. Good readers query the text as they read. What is the point of reading a mystery if you are not trying to figure out whodunit?

Students need to have intellectual risk taking modeled for them. Think-aloud protocols, common in kindergarten but much less so in secondary classrooms, can help students to see that reading requires more from them than simply passing their eyes down a page of text. This was brought home to me when I found myself haranguing a class of tenth graders for not doing their homework reading. I had asked students what they thought about the opening passage of George Orwell's *1984*, and not a single student looked up to respond.

"Why didn't you read last night's assignment?"

"But, Mrs. Jago, we did the reading!" they chorused.

"So what do you think?"

"You didn't say we had to think," a voice in back grumbled.

Dumbstruck, I realized that these able though not particularly motivated students did not see thinking as part of their reading task. I knew I had to make what should be happening inside their heads as they read more visible. In order to move forward we needed to take a step backward. I asked students to turn to the first paragraphs of the novel and to watch how I thought about the text as I read the page out loud. My commentary appears in boldfaced italics.

It was a bright cold day in April, and the clocks were striking thirteen. [*Hmm . . . why would clocks be striking thirteen? Feels ominous. But maybe it's just military time.*] Winston Smith [*Smith's a boring name. He's probably going to be a boring character.*], his chin nuzzled into his breast in an effort to escape the vile wind, slipped quickly through the glass doors of Victory Mansions [*Sounds like a cool place. He must be rich if he can live in a mansion.*], though not quickly enough to prevent a swirl of gritty dust from entering along with him.

The hallway smelt of boiled cabbage and old rag mats. [*Not such a cool place. This is nasty. Maybe it's a run-down mansion.*] At one end of it a coloured [*What's with the odd spelling? Oh, don't British writers spell this way?*] poster, too large for indoor display, had been tacked to the wall. [*This is sounding like a tacky place.*] It depicted simply an enormous face, more than a metre [*That funny spelling again. And meter instead of yard.*] wide: the face of a man of about forty-five, with a heavy black moustache and ruggedly handsome features. [*Sounds as though he's describing Stalin.*] Winston made for the stairs. It was no use trying the lift. [*Lift? Oh, yeah, that's what the English call an elevator.*] Even at the best of times it was seldom working, and at present the electric current was cut off during daylight hours. It was part of the economy drive in preparation for Hate Week. [***Hate Week?! We have Harmony Week here at Santa Monica High, but who would have a Hate Week?***] The flat [***Here we go again. Brits call apartments flats.***] was seven flights up, and Winston, who was thirty-nine and had a varicose ulcer above his right ankle [***Isn't thirty-nine young to be having a varicose ulcer?***], went slowly, resting several times on the way. [***Gosh, he does sound like an old man.***] On each landing, opposite the lift-shaft, the poster with the enormous face gazed from the wall. It was one of those pictures which are so contrived that the eyes follow you about when you move. [***I hate when the eyes in a picture do this.***] BIG BROTHER IS WATCHING YOU, the caption beneath it ran. (1983)

I then put students in pairs and asked them to think aloud as I had done as they read the next four paragraphs of *1984* together, pausing to ponder, query, and comment to one another about what they were reading. I also asked students to use a quiet voice as they did so. The room can become very loud very quickly during this exercise. I circulated among students, listening in to their conversations. After about fifteen minutes I brought the class back together to talk about what happened as they thought aloud and charted their responses on the board:

◆ Found words like *pig-iron* that neither of us knew.

◆ Figured out the meaning of words like *overfulfillment* and *telescreen*.

◆ Talked about what was going on in the story.

◆ Made connections to our own lives. Told stories.

◆ Had questions neither of us could answer.

As the bell was about to ring, I asked students to read the next chapter of *1984* for homework, replicating what they had just done with a partner silently inside their heads. More than mastering this protocol, what I want students to understand is how, in the words of Umberto Eco, "every text . . . is a lazy machine asking the reader to do some of its work" (1994).

Move 2: Practice Close Reading with Complex Visual Texts

As I modeled how I worked as a reader of *1984*, I purposely erred in an early inference, assuming a place called Victory Mansions would be luxurious. (Had I been a British student reading this, I would have known immediately that a mansion can refer either to a grand house or to council flats.) When I came to the description of the old rag mats, I realized my error and adjusted my visual image of the place. Students need to see their teachers taking interpretive risks and then revising their interpretation when a limb they've gone out on fails to hold. I find this easier to do with complex visual images than I do with stories or poems. It's hard to pretend that you don't know what a line means when you actually believe you do. Better to display a painting, photograph, or magazine cover and approach interpretation together with your students.

Visual artists approach their work with the same purposes as writers: to persuade, to explain, and to convey experience. The difference is in their tools. While writers employ diction, syntax, and imagery to establish a tone and convey their message, visual artists use color, line, shape, object, and scale.

Our students are bombarded by visual images yet rarely stop to analyze them. I'm not talking only of advertising. Media study units are popular components in many English syllabi. Less in evidence are lessons inviting students to read visual texts rhetorically. While many images—for example, photographs—have been ostensibly created to inform, they often contain powerfully persuasive messages.

In the same way that we challenge students to deconstruct and analyze a piece of writing, we can help students learn to "read" visual images. Invite students to look closely at a photograph like Lewis Hine's *Hartford Newsboys* (1909) for two minutes. It will seem an eternity, but insist on the full interval, telling students that if they think they've seen everything in the photo, they should scrutinize another corner. Sometimes I ask students to make a list of ten things they see in the image. There is nothing special about the number ten. I just want to keep students focused on the photograph.

I then ask students to turn to a partner and talk about what they saw. I tell them to choose one of the details from their list and explain to their partner why this detail drew their attention and what it seems to contribute to the photograph as a whole.

After about five minutes of discussion, I bring the class together to share what they have seen and thought. I ask students to think about how the title offers clues to reading the image. As the discussion winds down, I tell students about Lewis Hine's crusade against child labor and how his barrage of photographs from textile mills, coal mines, and urban streets appearing in newspapers across the nation resulted in laws forbidding child labor as well as more stringent enforcement of laws already in place. (As shown below.)

Such exercises with complex visual images build the same muscles that we want students to employ when they read a poem, a play, or a novel. They can also serve as an impetus to inquiry. Students inevitably want to know more about the issue the image raises. According to author Elizabeth Winthrop (2007), her novel *Counting on Grace* was inspired by a Lewis Hine photograph of a young girl standing in front of a loom. Though she was never able to discover any historical information about Addie

Hartford Newsboys, by Lewis Hine (1909)

Card other than her age, the image became the touchstone for Winthrop's story about child labor in New England textile mills. Another outstanding book for further reading is *Kids at Work: Lewis Hine and the Crusade Against Child Labor*, by Russell Freedman (1998).

Additional Images Ideal for Interpretive Risk Taking

◆ Norman Rockwell's *Working on the Statue of Liberty* (Appeared on the cover of *The Saturday Evening Post*, July 6, 1946.)

◆ Jean-Michel Basquiat's *Untitled (Fallen Angel)*, 1981

◆ John Singer Sargent's *Gassed*, 1919 (An image from World War I perfect for pairing with Wilfred Owen's poem "Dulce et Decorum Est.")

◆ Kadir Nelson's *A Day at the Beach* (Appeared on the cover of *The New Yorker*, July 11, 2016)

◆ Dorothea Lange's photograph *Children of Oklahoma drought refugees in migratory camp in California*, 1936

Addie Card, 12 years old. Spinner in Cotton Mill, North Pownal, Vermont, by Lewis Hine (1910)

Move 3: Demonstrate the Elements of Persuasion

As we develop lessons designed to teach students to identify and interpret rhetorical devices, it is important to make clear that *persuasion* is not a dirty word. Persuasion is an attempt to influence the beliefs and behavior of others so they see the world as we do. To accomplish this end, we often employ appeals to emotion as well as logic.

Following the Boston Massacre, Samuel Adams went to his good friend Paul Revere and asked him to create an engraving of the event of March 5, 1770, to be distributed in leaflets and newspapers throughout the colonies. The image was titled *The Bloody Massacre Perpetrated in King Street, Boston, March 5th, 1770, by a party of the 29th Regt.*

Ask students to look carefully at the iconic engraving and think about these questions:

◆ Who are depicted as the villains in this engraving? How can you tell?

◆ Who are the victims? What evidence can you find in the images to support this view? (You might need to remind students from their study of American history that the colonists incited the Boston Massacre.)

◆ What effect does the background architecture have on the engraving's impact?

◆ Do you really think that a poor puppy would be standing in the middle of the fray as the redcoats blasted away? Why do you think Paul Revere included a dog in the picture?

The Boston Massacre (The Bloody Massacre), 1770

The famous engraving is a piece of propaganda put out by our Founding Fathers, signatories to the Declaration of Independence. How is this possible? Pragmatism prevailed. John Adams, Samuel Adams, Paul Revere, and other revolutionaries needed to persuade their compatriots to commit treason. As British citizens, many colonists were understandably reluctant to do so. (My British husband calls the Fourth of July "disloyalty day.")

Paul Revere's image is long on persuasion and short on historical accuracy. A few of the details Paul Revere chose to manipulate include the dead man at the center of the fight. This was Crispus Attucks, in fact a black man here depicted as white, the first martyr of the Revolution. Nothing in the picture suggests that the Boston Massacre took place at nine o'clock on a cold winter night. So much for the blue sky. Despite—or possibly as a result of—these inaccuracies, Paul Revere's engraving energized anti-British sentiment and in so doing accomplished what it set out to do: persuade.

It used to be that the only images I could include in a lesson were the museum prints I collected or the dozen overhead transparencies that came with the textbook. Now with an LCD projector and an Internet connection, I have the National Gallery of Art and the Smithsonian Museum at my fingertips.

> *I often find that students are more willing to be bold in their interpretation of an image than they are with a written text.*

I often find that students are more willing to be bold in their interpretation of an image than they are with a written text. They seem more willing to believe me when I tell them I don't know why the artist made particular choices or what particular aspects of the painting mean. With written texts, students often hold back from taking interpretive risks, figuring that the right answer must be somewhere in the teacher's manual. They think I am holding out on them.

Analyzing photographs and paintings not only strengthens students' language arts skills but also prepares them for analyzing a world of news that is increasingly embellished with images. In the same way that a writer chooses to include or omit certain evidence, a photographer does much the same, choosing to point the camera toward certain things and away from others. Even without the trickery of Photoshop, cropping of a photograph can distort the meaning of a scene every bit as much as quoting a comment out of context.

Move 4: Avoid Instructional Moves That Don't Matter

In an article for *Principal Leadership* magazine, Michael Schmoker describes how, "for decades, we have embraced an ethos of 'more is more'—that an abundance of initiatives, instituted simultaneously, will result in a better education for our students" (2017, 42). His recommendation to administrators is to focus on prioritizing practices that have been shown to work. "Less is more. Simplicity and priority are jealous taskmasters. But if we exercise the discipline to stay focused on what is indisputably effective, students will benefit enormously—and soon" (43).

> *Many teachers feel like wind socks in a storm, sucked and blown back and forth by administrative initiatives.*

Many teachers feel like wind socks in a storm, sucked and blown back and forth by administrative initiatives. No wonder some of us choose to close our doors and wait for the winds to shift. But it is easy to lose focus even within our own classrooms. I know I have been guilty of inundating students with activities that might or might not always have resulted in a deeper understanding of the text. My file cabinet drawer overflowing with ideas for teaching *The Odyssey* definitely needs weeding.

Here are questions to ask when deciding what to embrace and what to abandon:

- What do I hope students will be able to accomplish at the end of this lesson that they could not already do at the beginning?
- Does the lesson offer many entry points for students?
- Do my directions send students back to the text?
- Is the amount of time students spent completing this activity commensurate with the learning they garnered?

Teachers tend to fall in love with the latest fashionable strategy and its accompanying acronym. Often these activities eat up time that would be much more productively spent reading, discussing, and writing. We need to focus.

CHAPTER 7

Losing Our Literature?

When I look back, I am so impressed again with the life-giving power of literature. If I were a young person today, trying to gain a sense of myself in the world, I would do that again by reading, just as I did when I was young.

—Maya Angelou

The claim that state standards documents discourage the teaching of literature and privilege informational text over literary works in English classrooms is untrue. The misunderstanding began when the Common Core State Standards document included a chart from the 2009 NAEP *Reading Framework* in its introduction. The chart, which includes the percentages for informational and literary text to appear on the NAEP reading assessment, was widely misinterpreted as a recommendation for the balance of information and literary text to be taught in English classes.

The numbers were never meant to stipulate that 70 percent of what students read in an English class should be informational text. They reflected the opinion of the NAEP *Reading Framework* panel that a large percentage of what students read throughout their school day should be nonfiction. Unfortunately, for many secondary students, the only reading they do all day happens in English class. Too many young people graduate without having read a single work of history, biography, sociology, economics, or science.

This misreading of the NAEP chart caused a fierce backlash among many English teachers. One English department had T-shirts made that read, "We are the 30%," on the front and a list of all the novels they taught on the back. There should never have been any need for resistance. As Advanced Placement language teachers and others have come to realize over the last decade, nonfiction texts that explore compelling topics can be extraordinarily effective teaching tools. Students are keen to read and talk about controversial contemporary issues. But this is not the sole responsibility of English teachers.

Disciplinary Literacy

Some years ago I was sitting in one of those beginning-of-the-school-year faculty meetings where we were arranged at tables with representatives from each of the disciplines. Each group was given chart paper and markers and asked to discuss the key obstacles to student achievement. Our conversations ranged widely. At the end of the allotted time, groups posted charts summarizing their discussions around the cafeteria walls. At the top of every list was a single word: reading.

We didn't know how to solve the problem we had identified, however. After all, none of us was an expert at reading; we were English, history, music, art, science, and math teachers. Avoiding the elephant in the room, we changed the bell schedule and passed a no-hat policy. As a result of this evasion, content area teachers—apart from honors and AP teachers—all but abandoned their textbooks, deciding instead to present material via lecture, PowerPoint presentations, and video. Why ask students to read when they couldn't? As a result of this move on the part of their teachers, our students' reading skills (again, apart from honors and AP students) declined. Those who had less got less.

Because texts are read so differently across the disciplines, students need to be taught how to approach assigned readings with lenses specific to the field.

Timothy and Cynthia Shanahan's (2017) research into disciplinary literacy found that content area teachers are best able to teach students how to read in their particular disciplines. Because texts are read so differently across the disciplines, students need to be taught how to approach assigned readings with lenses specific to the field. For example, evaluating alternative perspectives is essential for reading history but less important for reading in mathematics and science.

> Even the grammar of sentences varies systematically across disciplines. Linguistic studies, for instance, reveal that science writing tends to have fewer verbs and more nouns, attributive adjectives, and prepositional phrases (for example, "gradually expanding cumulative effect"). Sentence reading is consequently a different experience in a science class than in a literature class. (19)

While generic practices for teaching students how to navigate their way through a textbook can be applied across disciplines, reading laboratory reports and historical documents is very different from reading a novel. Science and history teachers have clear expectations of what they want students to learn from their reading, and those expectations bear little resemblance to what English teachers want students to experience when reading a poem.

Sam Wineburg, a Stanford professor who for the past twenty years has been studying how students learn history, believes that we need to teach students to read like historians, not to prepare them to be professional historians but precisely because most of them won't become historians. When students are taught to employ the approaches historians, use as they read documentary records from a historical moment (diary entries, maps, executive orders, newspaper headlines, speeches, and the like), students develop a sense of what it means to think like an historian. Students need practice processing information from various sources and evaluating that information in light of what they know about the source. They also need to acquire the habit of seeking corroboration for what they read, questioning conflicting details, and looking for areas of disagreement.

In an address to the American Association for State and Local History, Wineburg explained why teaching students how to read critically is so important.

> Reliable information is to civic intelligence what clean air and clean water are to public health. Long before the Internet, long

before blogs, before Instagram, before Twitter and Yik Yak, James
Madison understood what was at stake when people cannot tell the
difference between credible information and shameless bluff. "A
popular government," Madison wrote, "without popular information, or the means of acquiring it, is but a Prologue to a Farce
or a Tragedy; or, perhaps both. Knowledge will forever govern
ignorance: And a people who mean to be their own Governors,
must arm themselves with the power which knowledge gives."
(2015, 16)

Content area teachers should roll up their sleeves and embrace this work.
English teachers are never going to be able to "fix" students so that they can be
successful readers in all their other classes. We don't know how. Though strong on
sonnets, I am embarrassingly weak when it comes to helping students read any kind
of chart or graph, data displays that are essential for understanding an economics,
psychology, or sociology text. But efforts to persuade content area teachers to be
teachers of reading have been largely unsuccessful. Pressing secondary instructors
to teach generic reading strategies has neither been widely accepted nor particularly
effective in raising reading achievement.

NAEP scores in eighth-grade reading (where, remember,
70 percent of the texts students are asked to read are informational) were two points lower in 2015 than in 2013. Only
34 percent of eighth graders scored at or above proficient in
reading. Reading scores in 2015 for twelfth graders remained
essentially the same as they were in 2013 but significantly
lower than they were in 1992. This is not good news. When
only 37 percent of twelfth graders score at proficient and
above levels, it is time to take Tim and Cynthia Shanahan's
conclusion to heart:

> *NAEP scores in eighth-grade reading (where, remember, 70 percent of the texts students are asked to read are informational) were two points lower in 2015 than in 2013.*

As students move through school, reading and writing instruction
should become increasingly disciplinary, reinforcing and supporting
student performance with the kinds of texts and interpretive
standards that are needed in the various disciplines or subjects.
(2008, 57)

Though I used to think so, it simply is not true that if you can read *Hamlet*, you
can read anything.

Reading History and Science

I realize I am preaching to the choir here when I urge that responsibility for developing students' reading skills should be shared among all teachers. I am also sympathetic to history and science teachers' complaint that they have an enormous amount of content to cover. They insist that their bursting curriculum has no room for anything else. But part of the reason content area teachers face an uphill battle has to do with students' lack of interest in their subject. What if reading books about the topics being taught inspired students to want to know more? What if these books raised questions that teenagers were keen to have answered and triggered conversations about real-world implications and applications of what they were learning in class?

Publishers are doing a remarkable job of producing nonfiction books written with young readers in mind. Talented authors like Phillip Hoose, Gail Jarrow, Russell Freedman, Nancy Castaldo, Steve Sheinkin, Candace Fleming, Albert Marin, Susan Campbell Bartoletti, and many others are producing a steady stream of history and science books that both inform and inspire. These books don't talk down to readers. They do include photographs, primary documents, and visually compelling data displays that help provide context and complement the content.

As someone who has often found history books a bit too long and heavy on details, I find these books intended for young readers are exactly the right grain size for my own reading. I believe they would be well received not only by middle school readers but also by high school students. Take, for example, Neal Bascomb's *The Nazi Hunters: How a Team of Spies and Survivors Captured the World's Most Notorious Nazi* (2013), describing the harrowing tale of the capture of Adolph Eichman in Argentina. Bascomb had researched this story and published a four-hundred-page adult version called *Hunting Eichman* (2009) four years earlier. In his adaptation for younger readers, the language has been simplified and the text shortened (256 pages), but the dramatic suspense remains. I could not put the book down.

In *Hidden Figures: The American Dream and the Untold Story of the Black Women Mathematicians Who Helped Win the Space Race*, Margot Lee Shetterly (2016) provides a similar example. A short two months after the adult version of her book was published and at about the same time that the movie was released, an edition for young readers appeared. The main difference between the two is length and the addition of many photographs that in my opinion beautifully chronicle the times and lives of these women. I would recommend the young readers' edition to any reader, young or old.

Nancy F. Castaldo's visually gorgeous *The Story of Seeds: From Mendel's Garden to Your Plate, and How There's More of Less to Eat Around the World* (2016) teaches young readers about where our food comes from and at the same time makes a powerful argument regarding the importance of seed diversity and the growth of genetically modified seeds. In order to support her argument, she needs to help readers understand a bit about genetics. Like all good science teachers, she attaches new information to students' own experience, addressing her readers directly, constantly posing questions to ponder.

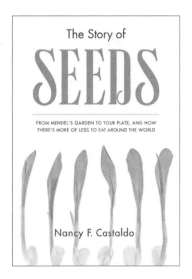

Hope Jahren's *Lab Girl* (2017) paints a remarkable picture of the life of a working young scientist. Winner of the National Book Critics Circle Award for Autobiography, Jahren describes her fascination with trees, soil, and science so lucidly and compellingly that I found myself interested in aspects of the natural world I never cared about before. She also offers a window into the world of scientific research. Any high school student considering a career in the sciences should read about the path Jahren has had to travel in order to conduct the creative research she is passionate about. She is also wickedly funny.

For younger future scientists, the Scientists in the Field series takes students into the eye of the storm with meteorologists and drone engineers keen to understand the dynamics of hurricanes (Cherrix 2017) and on an Amazon river adventure to learn about rain forest ecology (Montgomery and Ellenbogen 2017). Middle school students are likely to be stirred to action when they learn that unsustainable human practices are destroying 2.7 million acres—acres that produce one-fifth of the world's oxygen—in the region every year.

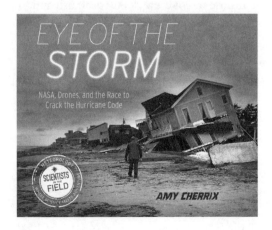

Clearly such books have the potential to augment what students are learning in history and science. They are more focused than the compendia of information presented in typical textbooks and as a result can include compelling details and remarkable images that seldom make their way into the larger tomes. They are also written with voice, an ingredient sorely missing from textbook prose. This example from the first two paragraphs of Jim Murphy's *An American Plague: The True and Terrifying Story of the Yellow Fever Epidemic of 1793* is a case in point. The book teaches the history of medical practice alongside the principles of infection and prevention in the course of a story that reads like a thriller. *An American Plague* was also a Newbery honor book.

> **Saturday, August 3, 1793.** The sun came up, as it had every day since the end of May, bright, hot, and unrelenting. The swamps and marshes south of Philadelphia had already lost a great deal of water to the intense heat, while the Delaware and Schuylkill Rivers had receded to reveal long stretches of their muddy, root-choked banks. Dead fish and gooey vegetable matter were exposed and rotted, while swarms of insects droned in the heavy, humid air.
>
> In Philadelphia itself an increasing number of cats were dropping dead every day, attracting, one Philadelphian complained, "an amazing number of flies and other insects." Mosquitoes were everywhere, though their high-pitched whirring was particularly loud near rain barrels, gutters, and open sewers. (2014, 1)

Compare this passage with the typical prose found in middle and high school textbooks. No wonder students are turned off from reading in science and history. Too many young readers have never been exposed to books like Murphy's that make the times and troubles come to life. Notice his use of concrete detail: dead fish and gooey vegetable matter, cats dropping dead. This is the same device that fiction writers employ to capture a reader's attention.

I believe such books might also pique the interest of students who would rather read about real things than made-up stories. Laurie Halse Anderson's *Fever 1793* (2011) is a carefully researched historical novel for young readers that in many ways addresses the very same issues Jim Murphy's nonfiction book covers. Her version takes a narrative approach, focusing on characters and dialogue rather than facts and figures. I know I am in danger of gender stereotyping here, but in my experience many boys prefer the nonfiction account to the novel.

I also believe that assigning one book related to the curriculum every semester in history and science classes would send a powerful message to students that reading is not just something they do for English class. What if students read *Fever 1793* in English and *An American Plague* in social studies? Or what about giving students the choice to read one or the other? Another pairing of a narrative and a nonfiction presentation of infection is Susan Campbell Bartoletti's *Terrible Typhoid Mary: The True Story of the Deadliest Cook in America* (2015) and Gail Jarrow's *Fatal Fever: Tracking Down Typhoid Mary* (2015).

Assigning outside reading often meets with resistance from history and science teachers because they are nervous about holding students accountable for their reading. No content area teacher wants to read a set of essays. Comprehension quizzes are quick and easy to grade but often miss the point of why we want students to read. They can also encourage cheating. A simple solution is to set a deadline for students to finish their books and on that day to ask them to write for twenty minutes about what they have learned about history or science from their reading. I would make it an open-book assessment. Teachers could easily grade the papers as pass or fail.

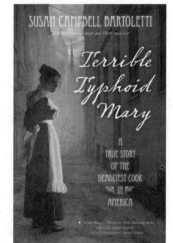

If colleagues in other disciplines remain opposed to assigning outside reading, English teachers can at least stock our own classroom library shelves with a robust collection of nonfiction titles and make sure that summer reading lists feature history and science books along with novels.

Outstanding sources of recently published nonfiction titles include the following:

- ◆ National Science Teachers Association Trade Books for Students K–12
- ◆ Notable Social Studies Trade Books for Young Readers
- ◆ Orbis Pictus Awards for Outstanding Children's Nonfiction
- ◆ YALSA (Young Adult Library Service Award) for Excellence in Nonfiction
- ◆ National Book Award for Young People's Literature
- ◆ Robert F. Sibert Informational Book Medal
- ◆ Andrew Carnegie Medal for Excellence in Nonfiction

I recommend perusing the lists of runners-up for these awards along with the winners. Very often, every one is first-rate. I rely on expert sources like these for nonfiction titles in part because I need to be certain that the information I am putting into students' hands is accurate.

When the Discipline Is Literature

English teachers often describe what we do as teaching reading, writing, speaking, and listening—the language arts. But we are also responsible for teaching literature, something no other discipline is likely to take up if we should abandon the work. Of course we need to care more about students than we care about the books we teach, but it is also true that students deserve to be reading, writing, listening, and speaking about works worthy of close scrutiny.

Many English teachers shy away from the classics, assuming that students will find contemporary tales more compelling. But it is often those stories that have withstood the test of time that, over time, resonate most for young readers.

Teaching classical literature does not mean dragging students kicking and screaming through works they hate. That way lies unhappiness for all. It does mean creating a sequence of lessons that anticipate where young readers are likely to have difficulty in a text and provide just-in-time scaffolding for their reading, scaffolding that over time comes away so that students develop confidence in their ability to navigate the novel on their own. My goal when teaching Shakespeare is that students may one day choose to attend a Shakespeare in the Park performance or find solace in poetry during times of trouble. Or write song lyrics that might one day earn a Nobel Prize for literature.

Much is made of the economic impact of education and how America needs an educated populace in order to be globally competitive, but of equal importance is providing tomorrow's citizens and taxpayers with an education that exposes them to the confounding complexities of world politics. Reading stories and memoirs by authors from cultures very different from their own helps teenagers prepare to live in a world that is increasingly interdependent. Teaching works of literature from across the globe invites these students to travel vicariously across time and place and to learn about other ways of life from the individuals who have lived and are living those lives.

English teachers need to take care when we present stories from other cultures not to characterize them as curiosities. The magical realist stories of Gabriel García Márquez are a case in point. If students only giggle at the larger-than-life corpse in "The Handsomest Drowned Man in the World" (2008, 247) without pondering the implications of the man's sudden appearance in this particular isolated village and the effect he had on the villagers, I fear we infantilize this complex short story. It is important to challenge young readers to see the irony of the story's subtitle, "A Tale for Children." Is Márquez being ironic or is he offering us a clue to the story's mythical nature?

In his 1982 Nobel Prize lecture, titled "The Solitude of Latin America," Márquez argues that while the Western world celebrates the outsized reality of Latin American literature, it has little patience with the politics of the region.

> Latin America neither wants, nor has any reason, to be a pawn without a will of its own; nor is it merely wishful thinking that its quest for independence and originality should become a Western aspiration. . . . Why is the originality so readily granted us in literature so mistrustfully denied us in our difficult attempts at social change? Why think that the social justice sought by progressive Europeans for their own countries cannot also be a goal for Latin America, with different methods for dissimilar conditions? . . . This, my friends, is the very scale of our solitude.

Rather than getting caught up in the fiction versus nonfiction argument, we might teach Marquez's speech alongside "The Handsomest Drowned Man in the World." Fiction and nonfiction should complement, not compete with, one another.

CHAPTER 8

Grasping Poetry

*Wasn't it strange that a poem, written in my vocabulary and as
a result of my own thoughts or observations, could, when it was
finished, manage to show me something I hadn't already known?*

Tracy K. Smith, US Poet Laureate, 2017–19

English teachers are often more successful at instructing students on the features of poetry than we are at demonstrating how to be readers of poetry. As a result, most students don't so much dislike poetry as simply find it annoying. The art form frustrates them. "Why can't the poem just say what it means?" they groan.

In his book *Beautiful and Pointless: A Guide to Modern Poetry*, David Orr suggests that our whole approach to teaching poetry needs rethinking.

> If there is one thing that unites academic treatments and how-to
> guides, it's the implicit assumption that relating to poetry is
> like solving a calculus problem while being zapped with a cattle
> prod—that is, the dull business of poetic interpretation is coupled

uneasily with testimonials announcing poetry's ability to derange
the senses, make us lose ourselves in rapture, dance naked under the
full moon, and so forth. (2011, xiv)

Reading poetry can be like visiting a foreign country. While encountering
unfamiliar customs at every turn, readers—like travelers—don't need to understand
every nuance to enjoy the journey. Sometimes the sound of a poem delights the
ear, for example, the rhymes and rhythms of "The Owl and the Pussycat." What
do Edward Lear's verses mean? I haven't a clue but cherish the way the sound of
the lines gives pleasure. Is it necessary to teach the definitions of *mince*, *quince*, and
runcible spoon (similar to a spork) before students can go to sea in that beautiful
pea-green boat? I would argue that it is no more necessary than it is to master the
language of a country in order to visit it. Students, however, do need confidence to
make the journey, something I fear a great deal of poetry instruction undermines.

Too often poetry lessons progress something like this: The teacher reads aloud
with feeling a poem she loves. Because this is a good teacher, she doesn't begin
peppering students with questions about imagery and diction but instead gently
asks, "So what do you make of this poem?" Silence. Not a raised hand in sight. The
teacher sighs and, because English teachers hate silence, begins talking. She tells
students about the poet's life and influences, points out where the poem turns, and
explains every allusion. Before you know it, the bell rings. Students shake themselves
out of their stupor and whisper, "Phew! For a minute there I thought we were going
to have to do something."

What pains me about this scenario, which I have myself enacted more times than
I would like to admit, is that students leave class thinking, "Mrs. Jago sure knows a lot
about poetry. Me? I don't get it." They wander off feeling both insufficiently smart
and insufficiently soulful—the exact opposite of what I want them to feel when they
read poetry.

Allowing Room for Confusion

Along with feelings of annoyance, students, particularly students who consider
themselves good at English, are embarrassed when they can't immediately figure out
what a poem means. Used to having right answers on the tip of their tongue, these

students are uncomfortable with the way lines of poetry make them feel inept. In truth, great poetry humbles us all.

I have read Robert Frost's poem "Acquainted with the Night"(2002, 47) many times and state here for the record that I do not understand now nor have I ever understood it. I do, however, respond with emotion to its extraordinary beauty. It is this beauty that makes me want to return to the poem again and again. I feel the same way about Frost's "Neither Out Far Nor In Deep"(2002, 62). Why do people on a beach always face the sea? What are they looking out to? What do they hope to see? The poem raises many more questions than it answers. By sharing our own uncertainties with students, we demonstrate how even accomplished readers puzzle over lines and struggle to understand the poet's intent.

> By sharing our own uncertainties with students, we demonstrate how even accomplished readers puzzle over lines and struggle to understand the poet's intent.

I like to invite students to close their eyes and imagine they are holding in their hands an object of rare beauty: a golden bowl, a newborn robin, a rose. Then I ask them to talk about what they would do next, how they would respond to the presence of this object. My students told me they would stay very still and look at it very closely. They said they would touch the object gently and observe it from every angle. Depending on the object being imagined, they said they would smell or taste or listen to it. Suggest to students that they try to behave in a similar way with a poem.

I purposely choose a poem for this exercise that is exquisitely beautiful and at the same time likely to confound readers at first glance, for example, John Milton's sonnet "When I Consider How My Light Is Spent."

When I consider how my light is spent,
Ere half my days in this dark world and wide,
And that one talent which is death to hide
Lodged with me useless, though my soul more bent
To serve therewith my Maker, and present
My true account, lest He returning chide,
"Doth God exact day-labour, light denied?"
I fondly ask. But patience, to prevent
That murmur, soon replies, "God doth not need
Either man's work or his own gifts. Who best
Bear his mild yoke, they serve him best. His state

Is kingly: thousands at his bidding speed,
And post o'er land and ocean without rest;
They also serve who only stand and wait." (1896)

I hand out copies of the poem and read it to the class. I then ask students to read the poem again for themselves, choosing a line that strikes them as luminous. We pause to talk about the meaning of *luminous*. As students finish reading, I instruct them to copy the line they have chosen and then write for four to five minutes about why they chose this line, about what it makes them think or feel. I give them permission to pose questions along with their comments.

When I see that most students have stopped writing, I put them in small groups with the following instructions:

◆ Have one person in your group read the poem aloud once more.

◆ Go around the group sharing your chosen lines and your reasons for choosing them. (I discourage students from reading from their papers, encouraging them to make this a conversation about the poem rather than a round-robin reading.)

◆ Collect questions that continue to puzzle you.

As I sense that their small-group discussions are winding down, I call the class together and read Milton's sonnet once more. I then call on individual students not to report out what their group has talked about (too boring and rote) but instead to share a lingering question or compelling idea that emerged from their conversation. I urge them to discuss what they see now that they didn't see the first time I read the poem to them.

You will have noticed that by the end of the lesson, students have heard or read Milton's sonnet four times. Teachers know the value of rereading for comprehension, but assigning a poem for students to read four times for homework will never work. I trick them into reading Milton's sonnet multiple times by creating different purposes and attaching difference voices to each reading.

Some versions of Milton's sonnet are popularly titled "On His Blindness," but that wasn't the poet's doing. The title was appended for a posthumous collection of Milton's work one hundred years later. "On His Blindness" offers an important clue to interpretation, however, particularly for readers unaware that Milton had been losing his sight, most probably from glaucoma, for years and was completely blind by the time he wrote this poem. Biographical details are not always important to a poem's meaning, but in this case they offer critical clues.

It is also worth drawing students' attention to Milton's allusion to the parable of the talents (Matthew 25:14; New American Standard Bible), where a man setting out on a journey gives his servants a number of talents or coins, "each according to his several ability." What is interesting is that this parable is considered the origin of the use of the word *talent* to mean a gift or skill in English. Milton's line is comprehensible without knowledge of the biblical reference yet enriched once you know it.

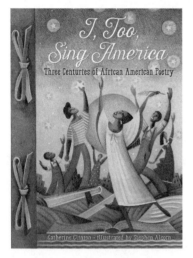

For homework, I hand out copies of Countee Cullen's sonnet "Yet Do I Marvel" (2013, 14) and ask students to take what they have learned about reading poetry from John Milton's poem and apply it to their reading of a poem from the Harlem Renaissance. I offer the following questions not for students to answer in writing but rather to stimulate their thinking and prod them toward making comparisons between the two poems.

◆ Where do you find similarities in how both Milton and Cullen question God's intentions?

◆ Where do you see differences?

◆ What is "curious" about making a poet black and bidding him "to sing" (write poems)?

Other poems that work well in this thematic collection include the following:

◆ "Sympathy," by Paul Laurence Dunbar

◆ "Caged Bird," by Maya Angelou

◆ "The Tyger," by William Blake

Perhaps I am being fanciful, but I hear echoes from William Blake's line "What dread hand? & what dread feet?" in Cullen's line "What awful brain compels His awful hand." This comparison also invites a discussion about the original meaning of *awful* as "full of awe" as compared with the conversational meaning we now attach to the word.

The Poetry Foundation website is a great source for many of the poems I mention here. I believe it is the most reliable source not only for accurate versions of poems but also for a plethora of resources about poets and their craft. You can often find an audio version of a poem read by the poet him- or herself. One of my favorites is Seamus Heaney reading "Digging."

Teaching poetry often feels like walking a tightrope. Too much teaching and students are intimidated; too little and they are lost. I want students to hold a poem in their hands the way they held their imagined precious object, to feel a poem's beauty before worrying about what it means. I don't want them putting gold frames around poems with the label "Great Art" but rather to see for themselves by looking closely, carefully, lovingly at what is there to behold.

Reading Poetry from the Inside Out

Another way to help students develop confidence in reading poetry is to have them write poems of their own modeled after a master's. My goal here is to teach students how a poem works from the inside out—by examining its moving parts and understanding their collective function. For this exercise, Wisława Szymborska's "Some Like Poetry" (1995) is ideal. In each of the poem's three stanzas Szymborska explores one of the three words from her title. Stanza 1 offers a definition of *some*, stanza 2 describes what it means to *like*, and the final stanza explores what *poetry* means.

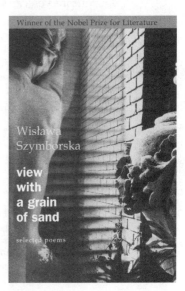

After reading "Some Like Poetry" and talking about its structure, we brainstorm three-word sentences of our own, filling the board with every idea that comes to mind. I suggest to students that shorter words will have more impact than multisyllabic ones.

- ◆ Dogs hate cats.
- ◆ I like cheese.
- ◆ Run with it.
- ◆ Do it now.
- ◆ Eat more fruit.
- ◆ Go to bed.
- ◆ I see you.
- ◆ Use your head.

Giving students only a few moments to choose one of these sentences—or one of their own composing—for their title, I invite them to write a three-stanza poem that uses each of these title words as the topic for a stanza. I ask them to look back at Wisława Szymborska's poem for inspiration if they flounder. They have permission to borrow any of her words or phrasings for their own poem. Here is a sampling of what my tenth graders wrote:

Truth or Dare
by Denver Hutt

Truth—
That means you can't lie.
Be honest, exposed, uncovered.
Bare it and smile.

Or—
There's your option.
Choose one, and if not that one,
Then the other.
But only from those two.

Dare—
Take a chance
A risk, a shot in the dark.
Do something you wouldn't
Under different circumstances.
And like it.

Light the Fire
by Nick Antrilli

Light—
That means not dark,
But not bright.
Just enough to guide you through the night.
Make a spark
To show you to safety.

The—
Ties the words together
Completes the phrase
Eat the food, love the girl
Each incomplete without the "the."

Fire—
But there are many types:
Passion, anger, jealousy,
This fire that guides us
Is in my heart.

I Like Sloths
by Peter Pak

I—
That's a letter in the alphabet.
But it could also mean "me."
It's a pretty general term.
One can say anything after "I."
"I go to school, I smell great, I *am* great."

Like—
What kind of word is that?
It's between loving and not caring.
It's a very weak word.
One can like candy, or one can like a friend.
It is used much too much.

Sloths—
What the heck is a sloth?
Maybe it's a type of Cajun delicacy.
Maybe it's a fungus.
Maybe it's a form of living booger.
Maybe "sloth" refers to 507 species of slow-moving, arboreal mammals of the
family Bradypodidae that are found principally in the rain forests of Central and
South America.
Who knows?

I was struck by the way students instinctively managed to capture in their poems both Szymborska's playfulness as well as her profound earnestness. As you might imagine, they could not wait to share what they had written with one another, laughing, clapping, and having a good time, all the while absorbing an understanding of how the poem works.

Teachers often ask me how I grade these style-imitation poems. Students never ask. They seem to know that some of their poems are better than others but don't feel it necessary to have their work rated. I give everyone credit for effort. It is important, though, to draw students' attention to the features that make some of their poems work so well. Together we talked about Denver Hutt's line from "Truth or Dare," where she wrote, "Take a chance / A risk, a shot in the dark," noting how she developed her idea through elaboration.

"Is that what you intended, Denver?" I asked.

Denver smiled and shrugged. "I guess."

"It's beautiful," the girl sitting next to her said with a sigh.

Who needs an A after a response like that? The goal of the lesson was to dispel students' fear of poetry and learn about the craft of poetry writing. In addition, I wanted to expose students to Nobel Laureate Wisława Szymborska. After using "Some Like Poetry" as a mentor text, they were keen to read more of Szymborska's work and to learn more about her. We were extraordinarily fortunate to have a Polish-speaking student in class who was able to read the poems to us in the original and talk about where the translations did and didn't, in her opinion, hit the mark.

I described similar lessons for reading and writing poetry in a series of books for the National Council of Teachers of English: *Nikki Giovanni in the Classroom* (1999), *Alice Walker in the Classroom* (2000), *Sandra Cisneros in the Classroom* (2002), and *Judith Ortiz Cofer in the Classroom* (2006). Modeling can take many forms, however. Students also develop insight into the hydraulics of a poem by borrowing the motivating idea behind a poem. Let me show you what I mean. In "Where the Wild Things Go," D. Gilson (2017) imagines what might have become of Max, Maurice Sendak's hero in *Where the Wild Things Are*, in later life. I begin the lesson by reading aloud the picture book to refresh students' memories. We then examine Gilson's poem.

Where the Wild Things Go
by D. Gilson

The night Max wore his wolf suit
made him infamous, bred the child star
never sent to bed. Middle school,
Max started drinking. *Not in my house*,
his mother begged, *No, no, no, wild thing.*
Max reminded her who bought
this condo, who paid for her meds.
Freshman year, Max raved. Roared
his terrible roar, rolled, and almost
wound up in a warehouse dead.
Where, oh where, do the wild things
go? To rehab in high school.
To college on residual book sales.
Max kept his head down. Laughed
at drunken frat boys. *Bro, let the wild
rumpus start.* Max said, *No thanks*,
and volunteered for the Peace Corps
instead. Two years in Kenya, one
in Belarus, the president thought
Max might be of some use. Max
moved to Washington, appointed
at the State Department a cultural
attaché. One important day Max wore
his wolf-gray suit, then drove home
well past rush hour in a freak snow storm.
Max drove on the deserted beltway,
thought it his throne. *Yes*, Max belted,
this is where the wild things roam.

I ask students to recall a character from a book they read or had read to them when they were children. It helps to jog students' memories by compiling a list of the many possibilities: the runaway bunny, Hansel or Gretel, amazing Grace, Freak the Mighty, Sylvester with his magic pebble, Olivia the pig, Peter Pan, Harold with his purple crayon. In the event that some students cannot recall such a character, I have at hand a tall stack of picture books they can browse that contain charismatic main characters. Their assignment is to write a poem in which they imagine what might have happened to this character in later life.

Before students begin to write I suggest that for their homework they refresh their recollection of the character they intend to write about. I give them full permission to change their mind about the subject for their poem if they come up with a better idea overnight. The following day we reread "Where the Wild Things Go," noting the number of times the poet has chosen to repeat Max's name. We also note places in the poem where he refers specifically to the original story, even borrowing the line "let the wild rumpus start." I invite students to do the same in their own poems.

This particular assignment lends itself well to an illustrated class booklet or online collection. Going public with student-written poetry gives students a reason to edit their work for spelling and mechanics. It also helps to make clear to them that I, the teacher, should not be the only audience for their writing. Once we have revised and compiled the class anthology of poems, I ask students to read the collection and write a note to three of their classmates whose poems spoke to them. As the notes pile up on certain students' desks, it becomes clear which of the poems in the collection were most successful. Again, a grade from me seems superfluous.

The Goldilocks Project

To become confident readers of poetry, students need to read many more poems than their teachers could ever assign. But how can we entice them to read without assigning more and more poems? Try the Goldilocks project. The guidelines are simple.

I bring into class all the poetry books I can find, everything from Kevin Young to Christina Rosetti, Octavio Paz to Billy Collins, Walt Whitman's *Leaves of Grass* to Claudia Rankine's *Citizen*. Most students have never seen books of poems by single authors and find the slim volumes appealing. I tell the students that I would like them to browse as many books as they like, looking for three poems: one that is too easy, one that is too hard, and one that is *just right*. Once they have chosen their three poems, they will write a short essay explaining why their just-right poem is just right for them, using the too easy and too hard poems as supporting evidence for their claim.

I warn students that I have not read every poem in these books and that they may come across one with language or ideas that offend them. If so, they can just turn the page or pick up a different book. I tell students to relax into their reading, browsing at will, and to let their just-right poem find them. The next hour can become a bit wild with students sharing poems they have found—sometimes for their beauty, sometimes for their shock value. They read dozens of poems in the course of the hour.

I ask students to copy the poem they select as their just-right poem and to include it with their essay. Students will ask permission to take a picture of the poem with their phone. Unless the poem is extremely long, I say no. Copying a poem is far from a rote task; it helps the reader pay close attention to every word, every comma.

On the day their Goldilocks project paper is due, I have students read their just-right poem to the class and explain what it is about this poem that made them choose it. I don't want students to read their essay—too time-consuming and dull—but because they have written on this very subject, most are able to present an impromptu explanation without much trouble. I find students are eager to find out which poems their classmates have selected. The lesson also introduces me to many poems that appeal to teenagers.

In a variation of this Goldilocks lesson, I have invited students to create poetry playlists. Teenagers are familiar with the concept of a curated collection of music compiled for a particular friend or occasion. Applying what they already know about putting together songs to poems is an easy move. We begin by listing the features of a good playlist:

- controlling idea or theme
- variety
- tone
- organization
- awareness of audience
- coherence
- purpose

I ask students to compile a playlist of six to ten poems, reading and recording the poems onto their phone. As with the Goldilocks project, I give them time in class to conduct their search from a wide collection of poetry books as well as from online sources of poetry. Before selecting their poems, I have students write a paragraph describing their intended audience for the playlist and what effect they hope it will have on listeners (bring them to tears, make them laugh, please a bird lover, soothe an aching heart, etc.). This moment of reflection helps direct their search.

Once students have chosen the poems for their playlist—this time I do allow them to photograph the pages with their phone—we begin the recording process. On occasion, students will ask if another student can do the reading for them. Why not? I tell the creators of the playlist to call themselves "producers" and their readers "the talent."

With thirty-six students in the class, it would not be possible for me to listen to all of these recordings, so I have students share with a partner as the designated reviewer. The creator of the playlist provides the reviewer with a list of the poems and the paragraph describing what the playlist is intended to achieve. After rereading the criteria for good playlists, everyone writes a review of the partner's playlist for my perusal.

Class projects like these help shift responsibility for learning from the teacher's shoulders to the students'. It is critical for students to be doing the work: reading, searching, sharing, and writing about many more poems than a teacher could ever assign.

Learning It by Heart

Now that even family members' phone numbers have been downloaded from our brains to our smartphones, you may think that having students memorize poetry is a practice that should have been discarded along with chalk and rubber-tipped pointers. Not so. Memorizing poetry is a powerful way to learn about the internal workings of a poem. It is also a contemplative task that can help to counterbalance students' much-distracted lives. As William Wordsworth wrote in 1808, "the world is too much with us."

In order to learn a poem by heart, you must surrender yourself to it, proceeding often with incomplete comprehension but trusting in the words. Memorization helps students understand the text they are working with because it forces them to follow the mind of the poet and to re-create the experience and feelings that went into the poem's composition.

This is not particularly challenging. Most teenagers carry around hundreds of song lyrics in their heads. They instinctively know how rhythm, rhyme, and repetition contribute to the ease with which a lyric sticks in one's head. Invite your students to choose a poem and commit it to memory. The Poetry Out Loud website offers a wonderful collection of poems ideally suited to the task. Poetry Out Loud also offers the following suggestions for memorization:

- Rewrite your poem by hand several times. Each time, try to write more and more of it from memory.
- Read your poem aloud before going to sleep at night, and repeat it when you wake up.
- Carry around a copy of your poem. You will find several moments throughout the day to reread or recite it.
- Practice your poem by saying it to family and friends.

To memorize a poem is to own it. Like nuts squirreled away for winter, the poems students know by heart will nourish them in times of trouble and provide company in moments of solitude.

It is hard to argue that the ability to read poetry ranks high as a college- and career-readiness skill. Many highly successful people never glance at any poem after high school. Job prospects for budding poets are few. Maybe as David Orr's (2011) title suggests, poetry really is just "beautiful and pointless." But then I recall stories about the Russian poet Anna Akhmatova. Though condemned and censored by Stalin, during the siege of Leningrad, her poems, passing from mouth to mouth, bore witness to the city's plight. Indeed, Akhmatova's poems came to symbolize the resistance, offering solace to the starving and succor to the suffering.

Maybe poetry isn't so pointless after all.

Students who can and do read poetry possess an ear for language that serves them well whatever the reading or writing task, from reading between the lines of an email message to writing a heartfelt note on Mother's Day. They develop an eye for words with nuanced meanings and for how such words can be employed for effect. They also possess a lifeline to some of the best thinking about what it means to be human. As William Carlos Williams (1962) reminds us, "it is difficult to get the news from poems yet men die miserably every day for lack of what is found there."

> Students who can and do read poetry possess an ear for language that serves them well whatever the reading or writing task . . .

CHAPTER 9

Asking Better Questions

Do those things that incline you towards the big questions and avoid those things that would reduce you and make you trivial.

—George Saunders

George Saunders spoke the words in the epigraph during a commencement address at Syracuse University. I find them apt advice for English teachers. We should incline toward asking students important questions. Good questions prompt thinking. They send students back to the text. They elude simple answers and suggest other questions. Unfortunately these are not the kind of questions many teachers ask.

Too often we ask students questions designed to check if and how well they understood what they have been assigned to read. A multiple-choice quiz on Chapter 8 of F. Scott Fitzgerald's *The Great Gatsby* asks:

1. Why does Nick believe Gatsby should disappear?
2. Who finds Gatsby dead in the pool?
3. Why does Daisy marry Tom?

Although such questions pinpoint important events in the story, their triviality insults students' emerging understanding of the novel. They reduce the responsibility of the reader to figuring out who did what to whom and why. If that is all that students take away from a reading of Fitzgerald's novel, it is probably not worth the effort.

Research on instructional practices conducted by Harold W. Stevenson and James W. Stigler suggests that the reasons that teachers ask questions in the United States are different from those motivating teachers in Japan.

> In the United States, the purpose of a question is to get an answer. In Japan, teachers pose questions to stimulate thought. A Japanese teacher considers a question to be a poor one if it elicits an immediate answer, for this indicates that students were not challenged to think. One teacher we interviewed told us of discussions she had with her fellow teachers on how to improve teaching practices. "What do you talk about?" we wondered. "A great deal of the time," she reported, "is spent talking about questions we can pose to the class—which wordings work best to get students involved in thinking and discussing the material. One good question can keep a whole class going for a long time; a bad one produces little more than a simple answer." (1992, 195)

One good question can keep a whole class going for a long time; a bad one produces little more than a simple answer.

I chaired the English Department at Santa Monica High School for sixteen years and confess that we never once invested department meeting time in crafting better questions. Looking back, I think this was a mistake. As an able and experienced group of teachers, we took it for granted that everyone posed strong questions that spanned the range of Bloom's taxonomy: remember, understand, apply, analyze, evaluate, and create. We knew we shouldn't be asking lower-level questions like, "What color was the horse?" Every one of us had seen at first hand compelling, higher-level questions sparking students' interest.

But we didn't closely examine the questions we were posing to students. A protocol for lesson study like the ones institutionalized in Japanese schools might have helped us better understand why some of us were more successful at engaging students in lively discussion. Rather than blaming our students or blaming ourselves, we should have been blaming the questions.

Questions That Send Readers Back to the Text

Architects of the Common Core coined the phrase "text-dependent questions" to distinguish the questions the new standards were recommending and that standards-aligned assessments would be including from the personal response questions they believed dominated classroom discourse. The term has become a ubiquitous tagline in contemporary instructional materials. As so often happens in education, we have taken good ideas—(1) that questions should be such that students cannot answer them without having read the text and (2) that they should send readers back to the text in order to scrutinize the passage more carefully—and turned them into something stupid. Suggesting that students stop making personal connections as they read makes no sense. It shouldn't be a matter of *either-or* but rather *and-both*.

Promoting text-dependent questioning was meant to be a corrective to instruction that began and ended with questions like, "Of whom does this character remind you?" or "Would you like Tom Sawyer as a friend?" While such questions can warm students up for a reading task, they also consume precious instructional time with conversation that sometimes has nothing to do with the text but is a personalization of the work under discussion.

We can write better discussion questions by viewing the text through three lenses: what it says, how it says it, and what it means. I want my questions to draw students' attention to each of these lenses in order. Of course, real classroom discussions seldom proceed as tidily as the phrases suggest, but I try to ensure that students understand a passage at a literal level before they begin speculating upon its significance.

I will use an excerpt from the first chapter of Linda Sue Park's Newbery Medal–winning novel *A Single Shard* (2002) as an example. The novel is set in twelfth-century Korea and its hero, thirteen-year-old orphan Tree-ear, dreams of one day becoming a potter like Min, the master craftsman. In this opening scene Tree-ear observes Min at work.

> Tree-ear made his way cautiously to his favorite spot, behind a paulownia tree whose low branches kept him hidden from view. He peeped through the leaves and caught his breath in delight. Min was just beginning a new pot.

Min threw a mass of clay the size of a cabbage onto the center of the wheel. He picked it up and threw it again, threw it several times. After one last throw, he sat down and stared at the clay for a moment. Using his foot to spin the base of the wheel, he placed dampened hands on the sluggardly lump, and for the hundredth time, Tree-ear watched the miracle.

In only a few moments, the clay rose and fell, grew taller then rounded down, until it curved into perfect symmetry. The spinning slowed. The chant, too, died out and became a mutter of words that Tree-ear could not hear.

Min sat up straight. He crossed his arms and leaned back a little, as if to see the vase from a distance. Turning the wheel slowly with his knee, he inspected the graceful shape for invisible faults. Then, "Pah!" He shook his head and in a single motion of disgust, scooped up the clay and slapped it back onto the wheel, whereupon it collapsed into an oafish lump again, as if ashamed. (1)

When asking questions about *what a text says*, I aim for areas where I suspect some students might not have understood or might have misunderstood what they read. I also draw attention to key details they might have overlooked on a first reading.

- What does it mean to throw a hunk of clay?
- How is it that the clay "rose and fell"?
- To whom were the pot's faults invisible?

Though some students might be familiar with pottery making and the workings of a potter's wheel, this context is so important for the story as a whole that I want to make sure everyone in the class can visualize the movements described in this passage. Too often inexperienced readers turn away from a book for lack of basic background information.

I encourage students to return to the passage before responding. My most able readers often have skimmed right past the sentence, "Turning the wheel slowly with his knee, he inspected the graceful shape for invisible faults," without considering that the pot's flaws are clearly visible to Min, who junks his creation in order to begin again, but invisible to the young Tree-ear.

Discussing Tree-ear's point of view regarding "invisible faults" leads us to examine the passage through the second lens, *how it says it*. We talk about how the story is told in the third person, yet we see only what Tree-ear sees. This method for telling a story is called third-person limited to distinguish it from a third-person omniscient point of view, where the reader knows the thoughts and feelings of all the characters. I ask students to reread the passage with a pencil in hand, marking places where the reader has access to events only through Tree-ear's eyes and ears. They then share what they found.

> **Kristin:** Tree-ear has a favorite place where he hides to watch Min work. He went there many times before.
>
> **Scott:** Yeah. In the next paragraph it says he watched for the hundredth time. That's a lot! Like years.
>
> **Ana:** And Tree-ear calls what he saw a miracle. It's a miracle to him but not to Min. Min junked the thing.
>
> **Kristin:** Something can't be a miracle if you make it happen yourself. This is how Tree-ear sees it.
>
> **Scott:** What's a paulownia tree? Can I Google it?
>
> [*I nod.*]
>
> **Jaime:** I didn't get the chanting.
>
> **Ana:** Min was saying or humming something while he worked. He knows what he was saying but Tree-ear can't hear the words. Is this what you were saying about a limited point of view, Mrs. Jago?
>
> **Me:** Exactly, Ana. Scott, what did you find out about the paulownia tree?

One of the hardest things to refrain from during class discussions is commenting every time a student speaks. There is always something I want to say. Far more important than my words of wisdom, however, is the maintenance of the natural rhythm of conversation among students.

Our exploration of what Linda Sue Park's first chapter says and how the text says it lays the groundwork for a later discussion about *what it means*. As the story develops, Min takes on Tree-ear as his apprentice. Theirs is a complex relationship.

A poor way to help students consider Min's treatment of Tree-ear would be to ask, "Would you want to work for Min?" The question is absurd. One may as well ask, "Would you like to be an orphan living under a bridge?" This is the type of question that gives reader response a bad name.

Instead, ask students to consider the significance of *A Single Shard* by having them reflect upon the ethical dilemmas Tree-ear faces over the course of the novel. What do Tree-ear's responses to difficulty reveal about his character? What can we learn from his story? Response questions like these direct students back to the text to consider the reasons for reading a story about a twelfth-century Korean potter. How do Tree-ear's trials inspire and even chide us? What does Linda Sue Park's tale have to teach us?

Most teenage students respond with youthful passion to moral questions. Literature offers young readers a context for examining the decisions characters make in the light of their own beliefs and experiences. These conversations are the reward for the hard work of close reading.

Questions to Help Students Engage with Complex Text

The first paragraph of a novel is often the most carefully crafted prose passage in the entire work. Along with being heavily invested with meaning and perfectly polished for craft, the opening can also be very hard to understand, not just for inexpert readers but for anyone. We come to the page with no knowledge of who or what or where the story is taking place (unless we have read a review, which raises a whole set of other issues). Trying to get one's bearings can be more than students can attempt. They need good questions to help them draw inferences from the details they are reading.

In Leslie Marmon Silko's *Ceremony*, the main character Taro returns from World War II deeply scarred by his experiences in a Japanese prisoner-of-war camp.

> Tayo didn't sleep well that night. He tossed in the old iron bed, and the coiled springs kept squeaking even after he lay still again, calling

up humid dreams of black night and loud voices rolling him over and over again like debris caught in a flood. Tonight the singing had come first, squeaking out of the iron bed, a man singing in Spanish, the melody of a familiar love song, two words again and again, "*Y volveré.*" Sometimes the Japanese voices came first, angry and loud, pushing the song far away, and then he could hear the shift in his dreaming, like a slight afternoon wind changing its direction, coming less and less from the south, moving into the west, and the voices would become Laguna voices, and he could hear Uncle Josiah calling to him, Josiah bringing him the fever medicine when he had been sick a long time ago. But before Josiah could come, the fever voices would drift and whirl and emerge again—Japanese soldiers shouting orders to him, suffocating damp voices that drifted out in the jungle steam, and he heard the women's voices then; they faded in and out until he was frantic because he thought the Laguna words were his mother's, but when he was about to make out the meaning of the words, the voice suddenly broke into a language he could not understand; and it was then that all the voices were drowned by the music—loud, loud music from a big juke box, its flashing red and blue lights pulling the darkness closer. (2006, 5–6)

The density of Silko's prose is hypnotic, and I want students to fall under her storytelling spell. I don't want them to sit stupefied and wait for me to tell them what the author means. Students need to do the work of close reading for themselves. My role is to convince them the result will be worth their effort. I also need to demonstrate that with a little help and concerted effort, they can do this work. Reading *Ceremony* poses textual challenges for any reader, but it is a text worth the trouble.

But how can we avoid overwhelming seventeen-year-old readers when the book is this difficult? Most know little about the Bataan death march and less about Laguna Pueblo traditions. Lecturing kids on missing background knowledge tends to put them to sleep. Having them research these topics takes up time I want to reserve for reading. It would also be misguided to introduce the novel by asking students, "Have you ever had a hard time falling asleep? Turn to a partner and talk about how it felt and what you did." Such activities might be engaging for teenagers who welcome any opportunity to talk about themselves, but they would accomplish very little in terms of preparing them for reading *Ceremony*.

Instead, I read the novel's opening passage to students. Listening first helps them hear the rhythm of Silko's language. I translate *Y volveré* ("And I'll be back") in the course of the reading. If students do not have their own copy of the book to mark in, I give them a copy of the passage to reread with a pen in hand. I ask students to note details that point to Taro's state of mind. Afterward, we note and discuss the phrases they marked. After every student contribution, I push students to explain what these lines reveal about Taro, asking questions like these:

- What does the phrase you chose, "humid dreams of black night and loud voices" suggest about the kind of night Taro is having?

- Why did you underline "He tossed in the old iron bed . . . rolling him over and over again like debris caught in a flood"? What picture did this create in your mind?

- You circled the word *frantic*. Can you find evidence of frantic behavior in the paragraph?

Reading the first paragraph of *Ceremony* is intentionally disorienting. Understanding how Silko achieved this effect can help take the mystery out of the spell. We return to the passage to examine individual sentences. Without much prodding, students respond that Silko's sentences are long, convoluted, and hard to follow. I tell them to look more closely, displaying this breakdown of the sentences on the board:

1. Taro didn't sleep well that night.

2. He tossed in the old iron bed, and the coiled springs kept squeaking even after he lay still again, calling up humid dreams of black night and loud voices rolling him over and over again like debris caught in a flood.

3. Tonight the singing had come first, squeaking out of the iron bed, a man singing in Spanish, the melody of a familiar love song, two words again and again, "*Y volveré.*"

4. Sometimes the Japanese voices came first, angry and loud, pushing the song far away, and then he could hear the shift in his dreaming, like a slight afternoon wind changing its direction, coming less and less from the south, moving into the west, and the voices would become Laguna voices, and he could hear Uncle Josiah calling to him, Josiah bringing him the fever medicine when he had been sick a long time ago.

5. But before Josiah could come, the fever voices would drift and whirl and emerge again—Japanese soldiers shouting orders to him, suffocating damp voices that drifted out in the jungle steam, and he heard the women's voices then; they faded in and out until he was frantic because he thought the Laguna words were his mother's, but when he was about to make out the meaning of the words, the voice suddenly broke into a language he could not understand; and it was then that all the voices were drowned by the music— loud, loud music from a big juke box, its flashing red and blue lights pulling the darkness closer.

◆ What do you notice about the progression of the sentence lengths in this passage?

◆ What does the increasing complexity of the sentences suggest about the progress of Taro's dream?

◆ Could the author be trying to induce in readers what the character Taro is experiencing? What purpose might this serve in terms of our feelings toward Taro?

> We often underes-
> timate students'
> ability to navigate
> complex novels.
> Just because they
> can't understand
> everything *doesn't*
> mean they can't
> understand anything.

Inevitably someone will ask if Silko purposely made successive sentences longer and more complex. (Students think teachers have magical access to writers' intentions.) I shrug and explain that artists do things instinctively that we lesser mortals can only wonder at.

We often underestimate students' ability to navigate complex novels. Just because they can't understand *everything* doesn't mean they can't understand *anything*. I know I don't fully understand Leslie Silko's novel nor will I ever. But I have learned from it and believe my students will, too. I do have to be careful when assigning books like *Ceremony* that each task I ask students to perform is doable, even seemingly easy. My goal is to build their confidence as readers. Students are too quick to equate puzzlement with incompetence. I want them to see lack of understanding as an indication that they need to study the text more closely.

Ideally students will begin asking themselves the kind of questions I pose to them in class. Such questions help readers break through the surface of the text, drawing attention to the clues that authors provide and sharpening readers' powers of perception.

Questions of One's Own

A seemingly easy but exceptionally powerful way for students to develop the habit of close reading is to have them write question papers. I am fairly certain that another teacher gave me the idea for this approach, but as with so many ideas, it has gone through the sausage maker in my brain and emerged in altered form. Question papers encourage students to explore the aspects of a text they find curious or confusing and to posit tentative answers to their own questions.

For this assignment students use writing as a vehicle for articulating their emerging understanding of what they have read. It isn't a matter of showing what you know but rather an invitation to discover what you can and to use what you find to figure out more. The task is easier to model than to explain. Act 5, scene I from *Macbeth* will serve as our prompt.

> **DOCTOR** How came she by that light?
>
> **GENTLEWOMAN** Why, it stood by her. She has light by her continually. 'Tis her command.
>
> **DOCTOR** You see her eyes are open.
>
> **GENTLEWOMAN** Ay, but their sense are shut.
>
> **DOCTOR** What is it she does now? Look how she rubs her hands.
>
> **GENTLEWOMAN** It is an accustomed action with her to seem thus washing her hands. I have known her continue in this a quarter of an hour.
>
> **LADY MACBETH** Yet here's a spot.
>
> **DOCTOR** Hark, she speaks. I will set down what comes from her, to satisfy my remembrance the more strongly.
>
> **LADY MACBETH** Out, damned spot, out, I say! One. Two. Why then, 'tis time to do 't. Hell is murky. Fie, my lord, fie, a soldier and afear'd? What need we fear who knows it, when none can call our power to account? Yet who would have thought the old man to have had so much blood in him?

DOCTOR Do you mark that?

LADY MACBETH The Thane of Fife had a wife. Where is she now? What, will these hands ne'er be clean? No more o' that, my lord, no more o' that. You mar all with this starting.

DOCTOR Go to, go to. You have known what you should not.

GENTLEWOMAN She has spoke what she should not, I am sure of that. Heaven knows what she has known.

LADY MACBETH Here's the smell of the blood still. All the perfumes of Arabia will not sweeten this little hand. O, O, O!

DOCTOR What a sigh is there! The heart is sorely charged.

GENTLEWOMAN I would not have such a heart in my bosom for the dignity of the whole body.

Here is one student's question paper:

I don't understand why the servant says that Lady Macbeth's eyes are open "but their sense are shut." I mean, shouldn't it be senses? But that wouldn't be right either because she is only talking about sight. Maybe she is saying that Lady Macbeth can't see OR hear them. I wonder how close the doctor and servant come to her. They would have to be pretty close, I think, because don't people just mumble in their sleep?

Why does Lady Macbeth count, "One. Two." Hasn't Macbeth killed more than two people? Isn't it a little late for her to worry about going to hell? I mean she's the one who told him to do it. She's the one who's tough. Even in her sleep she says, "none can call our power to account." So she's tough inside and out—but still has bad dreams. Maybe that's why she is afraid of the dark and needs a light by her in the night.

The dream is full of blood. Would Lady Macbeth have had to clean up the blood from Duncan's murder? You would think she'd have servants to do that but maybe that would be too risky. That would explain the obsession with washing her hands. I guess she's trying to wash away the guilt as well. She smells the blood in her dream, too. Maybe that's another of her senses that is off. Lady Macbeth sees and smells things that aren't there like the blood on her hands but doesn't see or hear things that are there like the doctor and gentlewoman. Maybe she isn't as tough as she thought she was. Maybe nobody is.

Writing freely about a short passage allows readers to range over the text, examining lines that puzzle them and trying out answers to their own questions to see if they stand up to scrutiny. My instructions to students are to write for twenty minutes without pause. I post the following sentence starters on the board in case anyone runs out of steam:

◆ I wonder . . .

◆ How?

◆ Why?

◆ It's possible that . . .

◆ Maybe . . .

◆ What if . . .

A question paper invites readers to think through a text without worrying about being right or wrong or concerned about arguing a position. There is no penalty for contradicting oneself here, no need to support a claim with evidence. It is a dialogue with oneself. Students enjoy the freedom of writing like this about literature so much that they often ask if they can turn in a question paper in lieu of an essay. To no one's surprise, my answer is no. I do suggest, however, that students might find it helpful to use a question paper to help them discover what they are most interested in exploring in their essay. It can be an effective first step toward constructing a thesis.

Questions with No Easy Answers

Asking good questions is at the heart of good teaching. The questions we put to students can either shut down discussion ("What action does Lady Macbeth perform continuously?") or open it up ("Why do you think Lady Macbeth repeatedly 'rubs her hands'?"). The first question simply checks to see if students have read the scene; the second takes that reading as a basis for discussion and invites them to explore the significance of what they have read. Which question would you be more interested in responding to?

I want students to approach literature with curiosity. Too many approach anything resembling a classic text with nothing but fear and loathing. They don't believe they are capable of reading Shakespeare. They are ashamed of their questions. How many times have you asked, "Any questions?" and been met with silence? Few apart from your most confident learners are willing to raise a hand and draw attention to what they don't understand. Yet these same teenagers can deconstruct the lyrics from the latest album and the subtleties of a complicated movie with great skill. They possess the power of analysis but are intimidated by the questions we demand they answer correctly.

Everyone misses things when reading, particularly on a first reading. Good questions can draw students' attention to important details they may have overlooked. The trick is to not make students feel stupid. Good questions point the way toward understanding. And once we have asked a question, we need to listen carefully to students' responses. Sometimes the most unexpected response contains genuine insight, albeit imperfectly expressed. Ask the respondent to tell you more and then listen hard. This may reveal something that you missed.

Questions are the keys to learning. They inspire students to look deeply into texts and, perhaps, to see more than they had ever imagined could be there. Composing good questions is the work of teaching. Listening to students respond thoughtfully is one of its greatest pleasures.

CHAPTER 10

Creating a Community
of Readers

*If you want to build a ship, don't drum up the men to
gather wood, divide the work, and give orders. Instead, teach
them to yearn for the vast and endless sea.*
—Antoine de Saint-Exupéry

Covering material in English class makes very little sense. No list of books or
set of skills could ever describe the outlines of what we hope students will
know and be able to do as a result of our teaching. For me, the ideal outcome
would be that my students should develop the inquiring minds necessary to learn
on their own. But how can we teach students to teach themselves?

Being able to learn on one's own is imperative for anyone hoping to thrive
in the decades to come. The rate of technological change is dramatic. Robotics
engineers warn of the imminent advance of artificial intelligence and the disruption
these thinking machines will have upon the world of work. While schools may be

doing a decent job of preparing young people for tomorrow's jobs, how well are we preparing them for the day after tomorrow? We can equip students for dealing with changes we can predict, but our predictions are necessarily limited. Over the course of their working lives, students are likely to hold a series of jobs in a variety of fields. In order to stay employed, they will have to develop new skills again and again. To do so requires a considerable capacity for learning.

Recognizing the Four Stages of Learning

Psychologists identify four stages in the process of learning:

1. Unconscious incompetence
2. Conscious incompetence
3. Conscious competence
4. Unconscious competence

In the first stage of unconscious incompetence, learners have no awareness of their inability to do something. Their lack of knowledge regarding the task leaves them blissfully oblivious to what they don't know. Picture any two-year-old with a scarf tied around his neck, pretending to fly. The child doesn't recognize the need to learn how to fly; he believes he already can.

In the second stage of conscious incompetence, the awareness dawns that the learner lacks the skill to achieve a goal, for example, riding a bicycle. With the awareness of incompetence comes the realization that new skills need to be acquired. This stage is often characterized by the recognition that others are more competent, thereby creating a desire to acquire the skill in order, for example, to ride a bike alongside friends. Training wheels, supporting hands, and a bit of a push all combine to propel the learner to stage three, conscious competence.

In the third stage, the learner can ride the bike, play the piece of music, or read the book, but doing so requires conscious effort and attention to the mechanics of the task. It is only in the fourth stage of unconscious competence that the learner can perform without conscious effort. Imagine the difference between a driver who has just learned how to operate a manual transmission and a truck driver who manipulates multiple gears smoothly and efficiently, unconsciously, enabling a clear focus on the road.

Most teenagers are consciously competent readers. They know how to read but doing so remains an effort. They haven't dedicated the hours necessary for automaticity to set in. As a result, they struggle in an Advanced Placement course and have difficulty handling the reading load at university. Such students often incorrectly assume that they lack the intellectual ability to stay the course. In fact, what they have yet to develop is the unconscious competence of an able reader.

Of course when the reading is particularly dense or the topic is highly technical, able readers know to fall back and employ conscious effort to understand what is being said. For example, I have no trouble reading a thriller with unconscious competence, but faced with this paragraph from a friend's blog, I fear I am back in stage two, conscious incompetence:

> Briefly, Kowarsky et al. take hundreds of blood samples collected from tens of patients, and use shotgun sequencing and assembly strategies to recover contigs from cell-free DNA. They remove sequences that match to the human genome, and investigate what is there in the remaining contigs. The authors also validate some of their findings by performing independent bench experiments, which is very nice to see since unfortunately 'omics findings are rarely validated by additional experiments. (Eren 2017)

I find it ironic that my microbiologist friend is writing in what he considers an informal, even lighthearted tone. That I can sense. It's what he is saying about the experiment that leaves me scratching my head.

Nurturing Autodidacts

An autodidact is a person who has been predominantly self-taught. Such individuals typically possess an enormous thirst for learning and often find school tedious, confident as they are in their ability to learn on their own. Terry Pratchett, whose fantasy novels have sold over eighty-five million copies, never attended university and said he felt sorry for anyone who had. Ray Bradbury insisted that his education took place in the library, reading, reading, reading. The late great playwright August Wilson dropped out of school in ninth grade but continued to learn by spending long hours reading in the Pittsburgh public library.

I don't want to pretend that many students possess the creative genius of Pratchett, Bradbury, or Wilson, but I do believe students' capacity for independent learning can be nurtured. Too many equate learning with seat time, believing that as long as they earn credit for a course, they are acquiring an education. We are substantially responsible for this false assumption. When all that teachers demand is compliance, students never develop the intellectual muscles needed to learn for themselves on their own.

When students are motivated to learn about something they believe is important, their inner autodidact becomes animated. For example, as I noted earlier, many teenagers are passionate about social justice. A teacher's challenge is to inform students' thinking with facts. Consider how often they draw conclusions from media images and so-called reality shows. We need to offer them more reputable and trustworthy sources of information upon which to base their opinions.

Studs Terkel's oral history collections are ideal for this purpose. Though the books are long in terms of page count, the individual interviews are short, engaging, and easily read and discussed in a class period. Whether students read *Division Street: America* (2006), *Hard Times: An Oral History of the Great Depression* (2005b), *Working: People Talk About What They Do All Day and How They Feel About What They Do* (1997), or *American Dreams: Lost and Found* (2005a), they will learn that Terkel takes care to present many points of view. The juxtaposition of different voices tells the larger story about social conditions and injustices.

Working Toward Independent Learning

The Terkel collection I have used most often is *Working: People Talk About What They Do All Day and How They Feel About What They Do*. Though some of the jobs described in 1974, such as switchboard operator, seem oddly archaic to students, the interviews portray such a concrete experience of work that they transcend the particulars of any single job. Auto assembly line spot-welder Phil Stallings comments, "I stand in the same spot, about two- or three-feet area, all night. The only time a person stops is when the line stops. We do about thirty-two jobs per car, per unit. Forty-eight units an hour, eight hours a day. Thirty-two times forty-eight times eight. Figure it out. That's how many times I push the button" (1997, 134).

I hand out copies of *Working* and ask students to scan the table of contents to find five interviews they are interested in reading. I then have them copy the job titles on an index card and find someone else in the class who has chosen one of the same interviews. This is all a very noisy business, but what I like about it is that students come away with a sense of the richness contained in the volume. Teams of students then read the interview, discuss what they have read, and report back to the class with a summary of what this interview suggests about the specific job. Based on these mini-reports, everyone chooses another three interviews to read for homework. Often students become engaged in the collection and read many, many more interviews.

As our combined experience of *Working* grows, I ask the class what they are finding common to people's work lives. What are the differences? What makes for a satisfying working life? What thwarts a satisfying work life? As students talk, I chart their observations on the board. We read more. We talk more. After a few days of study, I invite students to think of someone they might interview about working: a family member, a friend, or a stranger. This is not a "learning about what I want to be when I grow up" project but rather a chance to investigate what it means to work and what it means to face difficult working conditions and injustices.

We then move into thinking about the future, the day after tomorrow, when they will be entering the workplace. I invite students for homework to research the effects of automation on the world of work, the benefits as well as the problems. Following are a few of the many articles on this topic that are currently available online:

- "Evidence That Robots Are Winning the Race for American Jobs," by Claire Cain Miller (*The New York Times*, March 28, 2017)
- "The Robot Revolution in Caregiving," by Geof Watts (*The Atlantic*, April 25, 2016)
- "The End of Work," by Ji Shisan (*The New York Times*, December 10, 2015)
- "Find Out if a Robot Will Take Your Job," by David Johnson (*Time*, April 21, 2017)
- "Why Robots Will Always Need Us," by Nicholas Carr (*The New York Times*, May 20, 2015)
- "Known Unknowns," by James Bridle (*Harpers*, July 2018)

Without my having to draw students' attention explicitly to the implications of these technological developments, they begin to consider what their own working

lives may be like. As they share what they found through their research first in pairs and then in larger groups, the conversations become intense. Students are learning independently of me, their teacher.

Working Toward Social Justice

A contemporary oral historian I greatly admire is Anna Deavere Smith. In 1992 Los Angeles was torn apart by race riots. When Smith's book of oral histories *Twilight: Los Angeles, 1992* (1994) was published, I felt it imperative to have our own experiences of those days enlarged by the voices in Smith's collection. Although the language of the script—the author performed the work as a one-woman show—is sometimes raw for classroom use and the testimony charged with racial overtones, I persuaded parents that the subject was too important for us to avoid or ignore. I made the case that for the sake of a peaceful community we needed to know what others were thinking and feeling. Again we followed up with an oral history project of our own. And again, these stories prepared us to understand and address the racial discord and misunderstanding we saw all around us.

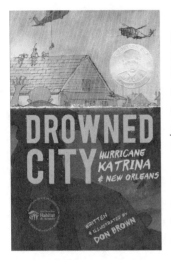

Anna Deavere Smith's latest work, *Notes from the Field*, is a play reflecting on education and the criminal justice system. In the play, Smith portrays nineteen characters, from Linda Wayman, a hardworking principal at a struggling Philadelphia high school, to Devin Moore, the delicatessen worker who videotaped police officers dragging Freddy Gray into their van. The script for *Notes from the Field* has not yet been published. I expect it will be an important oral history of our times.

There have never been any good old days. We are surrounded by issues that should not be ignored. I believe teachers are morally obliged to educate children for, in James Baldwin's (1992) words, the fire next time. Deep reading and courageous classroom conversations can help young people digest and confront disturbing news.

Making the Case for Speculative Fiction

Why do we need fiction, overwhelmed as we are by the unceasing stream of news and analysis? We need fiction because it increases our capacity for imagining the world from the inside out. Stories help us visualize the lives of others. They describe the complexity hidden beneath the surface of everyday occurrences. The same events appear very differently to different people. While reading fiction is no vaccine for small-mindedness, reading fiction makes it more difficult to remain wrapped in one's own cocoon. If the goal of public education includes preparation for the responsibilities of citizenship, I can think of no better vehicle than the reading of fiction. Stories inspire empathy. Without empathy there can be little hope of a civilized society.

Speculative fiction is often given short shrift in English course syllabi. Maybe this is a good thing. I would hate to take a true-or-false test or character quiz on George R. R. Martin's *A Game of Thrones*. On the other hand, judging the genre as too lowbrow for serious study excludes some of the most readable, compelling, and hair-raising stories I know. While science fiction and fantasy don't require chapter-by-chapter instruction, novels by Philip K. Dick, Cory Doctorow, Ursula K. LeGuin, Neal Stephenson, and William Gibson create ideal conditions for spirited speculation about the future.

I love the way in which speculative fiction encourages students to explore hypothetical scenarios and to consider the ramifications of what might *prima facie* seem to be a good or profitable idea. Consider Kazuo Ishiguro's novel *Never Let Me Go* (2006). What if scientists were able to clone human beings with the intent to harvest the clones' organs for use in heart, liver, and lung transplants? How would it feel to be one of the clones? What is the human cost of such medical progress? *Cui bono?* Who profits? As in most futuristic tales, readers find themselves weighing the advancements of science against their impact on characters they have come to care about. Ishiguro ensures this outcome by having the story narrated by a quite lovely and sensitive clone.

In a similar vein, Margaret Atwood's *Oryx and Crake* (2004) and *The Year of the Flood* (2010) forecast what could easily come to be, a world in which natural resources have been fully exploited or otherwise contaminated. Pets are gene-spliced life forms—a rakunk is a cross between a raccoon and a skunk—and a drug disguised as a prophylactic kills off most of the population. When we consider how best to prepare tomorrow's scientists, programmers, and engineers for the workplace, it seems to me that reading stories that lay out the potential fallout from today's ideas is a very good idea. Being a leader in technology and pharmaceuticals won't count for much in a world that is hardly habitable.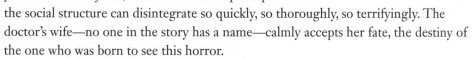

José Saramago's novel *Blindness* (1997) asks readers to imagine a surreal scenario and invites them to consider its implications for the real world. What if all but one of the residents in a city were suddenly struck blind? As society breaks down and the one eyewitness to the horror (an ophthalmologist's wife) leads her husband and seven strangers through a landscape that will remind you of Dante's *Inferno*, readers cannot help but ponder how the social structure can disintegrate so quickly, so thoroughly, so terrifyingly. The doctor's wife—no one in the story has a name—calmly accepts her fate, the destiny of the one who was born to see this horror.

Reading speculative fiction helps students to understand the world they live in and envisage that world distorted by apparent advancements. It helps prevent political blindness. In an article for *The New Yorker* called "A Golden Age for Dystopian Fiction," Harvard history professor Jill Lepore (2017) argues that many of today's futurist novels depict worlds that are not only paradise lost but worlds without hope. "Dystopia used to be a fiction of resistance; it's become a fiction of submission, the fiction of an untrusting, lonely, and sullen twenty-first century, the fiction of helplessness and hopelessness." While good science fiction sometimes frightens readers, it should not cause us to despair.

How and What We Teach Matters

The best thing about teaching is that it matters. The hardest thing about teaching is that it matters every day.

In an interview with Michiko Kakutani shortly before he left office, President Barak Obama said, "When so much of our politics is trying to manage this clash of cultures brought about by globalization and technology and migration, the role of stories to unify—as opposed to divide, to engage rather than to marginalize—is more important than ever." This gave me an idea.

This book is my attempt at helping teachers employ the influence they possess. We affect children's lives by what we say, by what we choose for students to read, by the books we surround them with, by what they see us doing and not doing. Teachers make a difference. We must decide the kind of difference we want to make.

In the interview, President Obama asserted that reading fiction helped him to imagine what was going on in other people's lives. He went on to explain:

> There's been the occasion where I just want to get out of my own head. [Laughter] Sometimes you read fiction just because you want to be someplace else. . . . There's something particular about quieting yourself and having a sustained stretch of time that is different from music or television or even the greatest movies.
>
> And part of what we're all having to deal with right now is just a lot of information overload and a lack of time to process things. So we make quick judgments and assign stereotypes to things, block certain things out, because our brain is just trying to get through the day. . . .
>
> I think that what one of the jobs of political leaders going forward is, is to tell a better story about what binds us together as a people. And America is unique in having to stitch together all these

disparate elements—we're not one race, we're not one tribe, folks didn't all arrive here at the same time. What holds us together is an idea, and it's a story about who we are and what's important to us.

No less should our classrooms be held together by an idea: the establishment of a cohesive community of readers. Within this community it is the responsibility of the teacher to foster an atmosphere of decency, fairness, and intellectual safe haven. It is a place where students say interesting things and then have those ideas challenged. It is an environment where readers demand that peers offer evidence in support of their views, a culture where controversy might rage but respect for one another triumphs.

Though teenagers have many other things going on in their lives—football practice, math tests, Saturday night—members of a thriving community of readers are always on the lookout for something to read. After all, what if your plans for Saturday night fall apart? A second responsibility of the teacher, the community elder, is to maintain the pipeline of books, providing easy access to a dizzying collection of titles new and old, classic and contemporary. Without having to be told, students talk to one another about what they are reading, sliding books across the table to a friend with a note that says, "I think you'll like this."

The third responsibility of the teacher is to select the books the community will read in common. Consulting with colleagues as well as with the community itself about these titles only makes good sense. Few mayors declare their One City, One Book selection without careful consultation with pertinent stakeholders. These books become part of the community's shared history. They offer a context for conversations about issues young members of the community are keen to explore but hesitant to raise. Fictional characters are invaluable facilitators of dialogue concerning delicate topics.

I am not describing cloud cuckoo land here. While this kind of a classroom environment cannot come into being automatically, a community of readers can be developed. This is a strategy. Not in the oft-misused sense of a strategy as a quick-fix trick but an approach to teaching that a general rather than a junior officer would employ. That is, a strategy that dictates the objective and charts the course the campaign, or community, will follow.

Creating a community of readers is work worth doing. Whilst the community will have its own momentum, the teacher can define or reset the preferences at any point. It is a genuinely creative endeavor, one that encourages growth in both teacher and students.

Appendix A

National Council of Teachers of English
Statement on Classroom Libraries

http://www2.ncte.org/statement/classroom-libraries/

MAY 2017

All students must be able to access, use, and evaluate information in order to meet the needs and challenges of the twenty-first century. These abilities are a necessary precursor to a sound education and healthy democracy. Reading in all its dimensions—informational, purposeful, and recreational—promotes students' overall academic success and well-being. Furthermore, when students possess the skills necessary to access, select, use, and effectively evaluate their reading materials, their ability to become engaged members of their communities and productive citizens is enhanced. A large body of research demonstrates that equitable access to books promotes reading achievement and motivation (Allington 2002, 2009; Krashen 2011; Nystrand 2006; Wu and Samuels 2004).

Classroom libraries—physical or virtual—play a key role in providing access to books and promoting literacy; they have the potential to increase student motivation, engagement, and achievement and help students become critical thinkers, analytical readers, and informed citizens. As English language arts educators, we know that no book is right for every student, and classroom libraries offer ongoing opportunities for teachers to work with students as individuals to find books that will ignite their love for learning, calm their fears, answer their questions, and improve their lives in any of the multiple ways that only literature can.

For these reasons, we support student access to classroom libraries that 1) offer a wide range of materials to appeal to and support the needs of students with different interests and abilities; 2) provide access to multiple resources that reflect diverse perspectives and social identities; and 3) open up opportunities for students, teachers, and school librarians to collaborate on the selections available for student choice and reading.

Administrators, teachers, students, parents, and community leaders are all essential in promoting, building, and maintaining classroom libraries, but teachers play an especially critical role. They are uniquely qualified to select books that

117

supplement and complement curricula and address the needs, interests, and concerns of their students. The National Council of Teachers of English supports efforts to provide teachers with the ability to exercise their professional judgment in developing and maintaining classroom libraries and to support them with financial resources to do so. The National Council of Teachers of English further strongly recommends that stakeholders do everything in their power to financially support teachers in their efforts to build classroom libraries.

Thus, as members of the National Council of Teachers of English, we recognize the specific educational benefits of classroom libraries to students because they

- ◆ motivate students by encouraging voluntary and recreational reading
- ◆ help young people develop an extensive array of literacy strategies and skills
- ◆ provide access to a wide range of reading materials that reflect abilities and interests
- ◆ enhance opportunities for both assigned and casual reading
- ◆ provide choice in self-selecting reading materials for self-engagement
- ◆ strengthen and encourage authentic literate exchanges among young people and adolescents
- ◆ provide access to digitized reading materials that may help to foster the development of technological literacy skills
- ◆ facilitate opportunities to validate and promote the acceptance and inclusion of diverse students' identities and experiences
- ◆ create opportunities to cultivate an informed citizenry

Furthermore, because classroom libraries serve the overall goals of education, the National Council of Teachers of English encourages teachers and other education professionals to

- ◆ recognize the importance of rich and diverse classroom libraries that offer students access to a wide and extensive repertoire of accessible reading materials
- ◆ promote students' right to read while recognizing teachers as curriculum decision makers in promoting their students' repertoire of literacy skills and strategies
- ◆ recognize that classroom libraries improve reading abilities for all students

◆ increase literacy resources for teachers through access to diverse mentor texts and opportunities to differentiate literacy instruction

◆ enlist other interested parties—administrators, support personnel, parents, and community leaders—to assist in the effort to financially support, build, and maintain diverse classroom libraries at all levels

Thus, the National Council Teachers of English supports, encourages, and defends the significance and preservation of classroom libraries in all disciplines in our nation's public schools and urges their continuation and implementation by classroom teachers, school administrators, and community leaders.

References

Allington, R. L. (2002). What I've learned about effective reading instruction from a decade of studying exemplary elementary classroom teachers. *Phi Delta Kappan, 83*(10), 740–747.

Allington, R. L. (2009). If they don't read much . . . 30 years later. In E. H. Hiebert (Ed.), *Reading more, reading better* (pp. 30–54). New York, NY: Guilford.

Allington, R. L. (2012). *What really matters for struggling readers: Designing research-based programs* (3rd ed.). Boston, MA: Allyn and Bacon.

Guthrie, J. T., and Wigfield, A. (2000). Engagement and motivation in reading. In M. L. Kamil, P. B. Mosenthal, P. D. Pearson, and R. Barr (Eds.), *Reading research handbook* (Vol. 3, pp. 403–424). Mahwah, NJ: Erlbaum.

Guthrie, J. T., and Humenick, N. M. (2004). Motivating students to read: Evidence for classroom practices that increase motivation and achievement. In P. McCardle and V. Chhabra (Eds.), *The voice of evidence in reading research* (pp. 329–354). Baltimore, MD: Paul Brookes.

Jacobs, J. S., Morrison, T. G., and Swinyard, W. R. (2000). Reading aloud to students: A national probability study of classroom reading practices of elementary school teachers. *Reading Psychology*, 21(3), 171–193.

Krashen, S. (2011). *Free voluntary reading*. Santa Barbara, CA: Libraries Unlimited.

Nystrand, M. (2006). Research on the role of classroom discourse as it affects reading comprehension. *Research in the Teaching of English*, 40(4), 392–412.

Reis, S. M., McCoach, D. B., Coyne, M. Schreiber, F. J., Eckert, R. D., and Gubbins, E. J. (2007). Using planned enrichment strategies with direct instruction to improve reading fluency, comprehension, and attitude toward reading: An evidence-based study. *Elementary School Journal, 108*(1), 3–24.

Scholastic.com. (n.d.) Access to books: Family and community engagement research compendium. Retrieved from http://teacher.scholastic.com/products/face/pdf/research-compendium/access-to-books.pdf.

Taylor, B. M., Pearson, P. D., Peterson, D. S., and Rodriguez, M. C. (2003). Reading growth in high-poverty classrooms: The influence of teacher practices that encourage cognitive engagement in literacy learning. *Elementary School Journal, 104*(1), 3–28.

Teresa, E. C. (2017). *Kids and family reading report* (6th ed.). Scholastic, Inc. and YouGov Parchilitam Kids and Family Reading Report 2017, Emily C. Teresa, Corporate Communications, January 30, 2017. Retrieved from http://www.scholastic.com/readingreport/files/Scholastic-KFRR-6ed-2017.pdf.

Trelease, J. (2001). *Read-aloud handbook* (5th ed.). New York, NY: Viking-Penguin.

Wolpert-Gawron, H. (2015). The importance of a classroom library. Edutopia. Retrieved from https://www.edutopia.org/blog/classroom-library-importance-heather-wolpert-gawron.

Wu, Y., and Samuels, S. J. (2004, May). How the amount of time spent on independent reading affects reading achievement. Paper presented at the annual convention of the International Reading Association, Reno, Nevada.

The NCTE Standing Committee Against Censorship, 2016–2017

Chair: Jeffrey Kaplan, University of Central Florida, Orlando

Christina Berchini, University of Wisconsin, Eau Claire

Joan Bertin, National Coalition Against Censorship, New York, NY

Jean Brown, Rhode Island College, Providence

Annamary Consalvo, University of Texas at Tyler

Brooke Boback Eisenbach, Lesley University, Cambridge, MA

Barry Gilmore, Hutchison School, Memphis, TN

Wendy Glenn, University of Connecticut, Storrs

Paula Greathouse, Tennessee Tech University, Cookeville

Yvette R. Hyde, Covington Education Center, Covington, LA

Sarah Willens Kass, Westland Middle School, Bethesda, MD

William D. Kemp, Albany, NY

ReLeah Lent, Morgantown, GA

Risha Leigh Mullins, Chandlersville, OH

Connie Nagel, Bettendorf, IA

Gretchen Oltman, Creighton University, Omaha, NE

Jonathan Rogers, Iowa City High School, IA

Kym Sheehan, Charlotte County Public Schools, FL

Appendix B

Suggestions for Your Classroom Library

Welcome to my list of suggestions for your classroom library. It is not meant in any way to be a perfect list. Only you know what titles will be most appealing to your students and which books might be problematic in your school community. I have compiled here a list of books that I believe can open up the world to middle and high school readers.

Some of these stories include scenes of violence or language that might offend. That said, I have read every one of these books and believe the scenes and language contribute importantly to the author's intent and message.

Thanks for all you do to bring books into your students' lives. Reading helps us be more fully human. In the words of the inimitable teacher Colby Sharp, "it doesn't matter how many books you have in your classroom library; it is never enough."

Note: I have indicated with a + titles on the high school list that I believe mature middle school readers would find engaging. On the middle school list I have indicated with an * titles that I believe many ninth and tenth graders would also enjoy.

AUTHOR	TITLE	LEVEL	GENRE
Hillenbrand, Laura	*Unbroken: A World War II Story of Survival, Resilience, and Redemption*	high school	biography
Isaacson, Walter	*Steve Jobs*	high school	biography
Kidder, Tracy	*Mountains Beyond Mountains: The Quest of Dr. Paul Farmer, A Man Who Would Cure the World*	high school	biography
McCullough, David	*The Wright Brothers +*	high school	biography
Pawel, Miriam	*The Crusades of Cesar Chavez: A Biography*	high school	biography
Stone, Brad	*The Everything Store: Jeff Bezos and the Age of Amazon*	high school	biography
Baldwin, James	*The Fire Next Time*	high school	essay
Berry, Wendell	*What Are People For?*	high school	essay

AUTHOR	TITLE	LEVEL	GENRE
Carr, Nicholas	*The Glass Cage: How Our Computers Are Changing Us +*	high school	essay
Cisneros, Sandra	*A House of My Own: Stories from My Life*	high school	essay
Oliver, Mary	*Upstream*	high school	essay
Rose, Mike	*Why School?*	high school	essay
Schwartz, Barry	*Why We Work*	high school	essay
Solnit, Rebecca	*A Paradise Built in Hell*	high school	essay
Solnit, Rebecca	*Hope in the Dark: Untold Histories, Wild Possibilities*	high school	essay
Ward, Jesmyn (editor)	*The Fire This Time: A New Generation Speaks About Race*	high school	essay
Williams, Terry Tempest	*The Hour of Land: A Personal Topography of America's National Parks*	high school	essay
Lewis, John, Andrew Adin, and Nate Powell	*March trilogy +*	high school	graphic biography
Bechdel, Alison	*Fun Home: A Family Tragicomic*	high school	graphic memoir
Samanci, Ozge	*Dare to Disappoint: Growing Up in Turkey*	high school	graphic memoir
Sattouf, Riad	*The Arab of the Future: A Childhood in the Middle East 1978–84*	high school	graphic memoir
Sattouf, Riad	*The Arab of the Future 2: A Childhood in the Middle East 1984–1985*	high school	graphic memoir
Butler, Octavia, Damian Duffy, and John Jennings	*Kindred: A Graphic Novel Adaptation*	high school	graphic novel
Anderson, M. T.	*The Astonishing Life of Octavian Nothing, Traitor to the Nation*	high school	historical fiction
Bagdasarian, Adam	*Forgotten Fire*	high school	historical fiction
McCormick, Patricia	*Never Fall Down*	high school	historical fiction
McCormick, Patricia	*Purple Heart*	high school	historical fiction

AUTHOR	TITLE	LEVEL	GENRE
Alexander, Elizabeth	*In the Light of the World*	high school	memoir
Castillo, Ana	*Black Dove: Mamá, Mi'jo, and Me*	high school	memoir
Coates, Ta-Nehisi	*The Beautiful Struggle*	high school	memoir
Didion, Joan	*The Year of Magical Thinking*	high school	memoir
Eire, Carlos	*Waiting for Snow in Havana*	high school	memoir
Finnegan, William	*Barbarian Days: A Surfing Life +*	high school	memoir
Gay, Roxane	*Hunger: A Memoir of (My) Body*	high school	memoir
Grande, Reyna	*The Distance Between Us*	high school	memoir
Hemon, Aleksandar	*The Book of My Lives*	high school	memoir
Huxley, Elspeth	*The Flame Trees of Thika*	high school	memoir
Jahren, Hope	*Lab Girl*	high school	memoir
Jefferson, Margo	*Negroland: A Memoir*	high school	memoir
Kalanithi, Paul	*When Breath Becomes Air*	high school	memoir
Kamara, Mariatu	*The Bite of the Mango +*	high school	memoir
Kamkwamba, William, and Bryan Mealer	*The Boy Who Harnessed the Wind +*	high school	memoir
Kim, Suki	*Without You, There Is No Us*	high school	memoir
Kincaid, Jamaica	*A Small Place*	high school	memoir
Kincaid, Jamaica	*Autobiography of My Mother*	high school	memoir
Kincaid, Jamaica	*See Now Then*	high school	memoir
Kristofic, Jim	*Navajos Wear Nikes*	high school	memoir
Macdonald, Helen	*H Is for Hawk*	high school	memoir
Noah, Trevor	*Born a Crime: Stories from a South African Childhood +*	high school	memoir
Petrushevskaya, Ludmilla	*The Girl from the Metropol Hotel: Growing Up in Communist Russia*	high school	memoir
Sacks, Oliver	*A Leg to Stand On*	high school	memoir
Shteyngart, Gary	*Little Failure: A Memoir*	high school	memoir

AUTHOR	TITLE	LEVEL	GENRE
Smith, Patti	*Just Kids*	high school	memoir
Sotomayor, Sonya	*My Beloved World* +	high school	memoir
Tretheway, Natasha	*Beyond Katrina: A Meditation on the Mississippi Gulf Coast*	high school	memoir
Turner, Brian	*My Life as a Foreign Country: A Memoir*	high school	memoir
Williams, Thomas Chatterton	*Losing My Cool: Love, Literature, and a Black Man's Escape from the Crowd*	high school	memoir
Abbott, Karen	*Liar, Temptress, Soldier, Spy*	high school	nonfiction
Alexander, Michelle	*The New Jim Crow*	high school	nonfiction
Bausum, Ann	*Stonewall: Breaking Out in the Fight for Gay Rights*	high school	nonfiction
Beah, Ishmael	*A Long Way Gone: Memoirs of a Boy Soldier* +	high school	nonfiction
Boo, Katherine	*Behind the Beautiful Forevers*	high school	nonfiction
Capote, Truman	*In Cold Blood*	high school	nonfiction
Carr, Nicholas	*The Shallows: What the Internet Is Doing to Your Brain*	high school	nonfiction
Carter, Bill	*Boom, Bust, Boom: A Story About Copper, the Metal That Runs the World*	high school	nonfiction
Coates, Ta-Nehisi	*Between the World and Me*	high school	nonfiction
Cullen, Dave	*Columbine*	high school	nonfiction
Danticat, Edwidge	*Brother, I'm Dying*	high school	nonfiction
De Waal, Edmund	*The Hare with Amber Eyes*	high school	nonfiction
Desmond, Matthew	*Evicted: Poverty and Profit in the American City*	high school	nonfiction
Diamond, Jared	*Collapse*	high school	nonfiction
Diamond, Jared	*Guns, Germs, and Steel*	high school	nonfiction
Dyson, Michael Eric	*The Black Presidency: Barack Obama and the Politics of Race in America*	high school	nonfiction

AUTHOR	TITLE	LEVEL	GENRE
Egan, Timothy	*The Worst Hard Time: The Untold Story of Those Who Survived the Great American Dust Bowl*	high school	nonfiction
Feynman, Richard	*Surely You're Joking, Mr. Feynman*	high school	nonfiction
Filkins, Dexter	*The Forever War*	high school	nonfiction
Finkel, David	*Thank You for Your Service*	high school	nonfiction
Finkel, David	*The Good Soldiers*	high school	nonfiction
Friedman, Thomas	*Thank You for Being Late*	high school	nonfiction
Goodwin, Doris Kearns	*Team of Rivals*	high school	nonfiction
Grandin, Temple	*Animals in Translation +*	high school	nonfiction
Greenblatt, Stephen	*Will in the World*	high school	nonfiction
Hersey, John	*Hiroshima +*	high school	nonfiction
Hohn, Donovan	*Moby-Duck*	high school	nonfiction
Johnson, Steven	*The Ghost Map: The Story of London's Most Terrifying Epidemic*	high school	nonfiction
Katz, Jon	*Geeks: How Two Lost Boys Rode the Internet Out of Idaho*	high school	nonfiction
Kidder, Tracy	*Strength in What Remains*	high school	nonfiction
Kimmerer, Robin Wall	*Braiding Sweetgrass: Indigenous Wisdom, Scientific Knowledge*	high school	nonfiction
Kotlowitz, Alex	*There Are No Children Here*	high school	nonfiction
Krakauer, Jon	*Missoula: Rape and the Justice System in a College Town*	high school	nonfiction
Kurlansky, Mark	*Cod: A Biography of the Fish That Changed the World*	high school	nonfiction
Larson, Erik	*Devil in the White City*	high school	nonfiction
Larson, Erik	*In the Garden of Beasts*	high school	nonfiction
Larson, Erik	*Isaac's Storm*	high school	nonfiction

AUTHOR	TITLE	LEVEL	GENRE
Larson, Erik	*Lethal Passage: The Story of a Gun*	high school	nonfiction
LeDuff, David	*Detroit: An American Autopsy*	high school	nonfiction
Leovy, Jill	*Ghettoside: A True Story of Murder in America*	high school	nonfiction
Lewis, Michael	*The Big Short*	high school	nonfiction
Lord, Walter	*A Night to Remember*	high school	nonfiction
Lynch, Thomas	*The Undertaking: Life Studies from the Dismal Trade +*	high school	nonfiction
MacFarquhar, Larissa	*Strangers Drowning*	high school	nonfiction
McBride, James	*Kill 'em and Leave: Searching for James Brown and the American Soul*	high school	nonfiction
Moore, Wes	*The Other Wes Moore: One Name, Two Fates +*	high school	nonfiction
Nemirovsky, Irene	*Suite Française*	high school	nonfiction
Osborne, Steve	*The Job +*	high school	nonfiction
Patchett, Ann	*Truth and Beauty: A Friendship*	high school	nonfiction
Pawel, Miriam	*The Union of Their Dreams*	high school	nonfiction
Phillips, Patrick	*Blood at the Root*	high school	nonfiction
Prose, Francine	*Reading Like a Writer*	high school	nonfiction
Reding, Nick	*Methland*	high school	nonfiction
Rivlin, Mark	*Katrina: After the Flood*	high school	nonfiction
Roberts, Jason	*A Sense of the World*	high school	nonfiction
Sacks, Oliver	*The Man Who Mistook His Wife for a Hat*	high school	nonfiction
Sandel, Michael	*Justice*	high school	nonfiction
Sands, Philippe	*East West Street: On the Origins of Genocide and Crimes Against Humanity*	high school	nonfiction
Shapiro, James	*1599: A Year in the Life of William Shakespeare*	high school	nonfiction
Standage, Tom	*A History of the World in 6 Glasses*	high school	nonfiction

AUTHOR	TITLE	LEVEL	GENRE
Stevenson, Bryan	*Just Mercy: A Story of Justice and Redemption*	high school	nonfiction
Terkel, Studs	*Division Street*	high school	nonfiction
Tovar, Hector	*Deep Down Dark: 33 Men Buried in a Chilean Mine*	high school	nonfiction
Turkle, Sherry	*Alone Together*	high school	nonfiction
Turkle, Sherry	*Reclaiming Conversation*	high school	nonfiction
Tyson, Timothy	*Blood Done Sign My Name*	high school	nonfiction
Vance, J. D.	*Hillbilly Elegy*	high school	nonfiction
Wideman, John Edgar	*Writing to Save a Life: The Louis Till File*	high school	nonfiction
Wilkerson, Isabel	*The Warmth of Other Suns*	high school	nonfiction
Wilson, E. O.	*Letters from a Scientist*	high school	nonfiction
Kolbert, Elizabeth	*The Sixth Extinction*	high school	nonfiction
Ackerman, Diane	*The Zookeeper's Wife*	high school	novel
Adiche, Chimamanda Ngozi	*Americanah*	high school	novel
Adichie, Chimamanda Ngozi	*Half of a Yellow Sun*	high school	novel
Adiga, Aravind	*The White Tiger*	high school	novel
Ahmad, Jamil	*The Wandering Falcon*	high school	novel
Al Aswary, Alla	*The Yacoubian Building*	high school	novel
Alameddine, Rabih	*An Unnecessary Woman*	high school	novel
Alarcon, Daniel	*Lost City Radio*	high school	novel
Alyan, Hala	*Salt Houses*	high school	novel
Amis, Martin	*Time's Arrow*	high school	novel
Anderson, M. T.	*Feed* +	high school	novel
Aslam, Nadeem	*The Golden Legend*	high school	novel
Atkinson, Kate	*Life After Life*	high school	novel

AUTHOR	TITLE	LEVEL	GENRE
Atwood, Margaret	*MaddAddam*	high school	novel
Atwood, Margaret	*The Blind Assassin*	high school	novel
Atwood, Margaret	*The Year of the Flood*	high school	novel
Ba, Mariama	*So Long a Letter*	high school	novel
Barbery, Muriel	*The Elegance of the Hedgehog +*	high school	novel
Barker, Pat	*Regeneration*	high school	novel
Beatty, Paul	*The Sellout*	high school	novel
Benioff, David	*City of Thieves*	high school	novel
Berlinski, Mischa	*Fieldwork*	high school	novel
Black, Benjamin	*Christine Falls*	high school	novel
Brooks, Geraldine	*Caleb's Crossing*	high school	novel
Brooks, Geraldine	*March*	high school	novel
Brooks, Geraldine	*People of the Book*	high school	novel
Brown, Claude	*Manchild in the Promised Land*	high school	novel
Carey, Peter	*His Illegal Self*	high school	novel
Carey, Peter	*Theft: A Love Story*	high school	novel
Cline, Emma	*The Girls*	high school	novel
Cline, Ernest	*Ready Player One +*	high school	novel
Crace, Jim	*The Pesthouse*	high school	novel
Cristof, Agota	*The Notebook*	high school	novel
Danticat, Edwidge	*The Dewbreaker*	high school	novel
Daoud, Kamel	*The Mersault Investigations*	high school	novel
de Vigan, Delphine	*No and Me +*	high school	novel
DeLillo, Don	*Zero K*	high school	novel
Dessai, Kirin	*The Innocence of Loss*	high school	novel
Dimaline, Cherie	*The Marrow Thieves*	high school	novel
Doctorow, Cory	*Walkaway*	high school	novel

AUTHOR	TITLE	LEVEL	GENRE
Doctorow, Cory	*Homeland* +	high school	novel
Doctorow, Cory	*Little Brother* +	high school	novel
Doerr, Anthony	*All the Light We Cannot See*	high school	novel
Donoghue, Emily	*Room*	high school	novel
Egan, Jennifer	*A Visit from the Goon Squad*	high school	novel
Egan, Jennifer	*The Keep*	high school	novel
Eggers, Dave	*A Hologram for the King*	high school	novel
Eggers, Dave	*The Circle*	high school	novel
Enright, Anne	*The Green Road*	high school	novel
Erdrich, Louise	*LaRose*	high school	novel
Erdrich, Louise	*The Painted Drum*	high school	novel
Erdrich, Louise	*The Round House*	high school	novel
Faber, Michael	*The Book of Strange New Things*	high school	novel
Federle, Tim	*The Great American Whatever* +	high school	novel
Ferris, Joshua	*Then We Came to the End*	high school	novel
Ford, Jamie	*Hotel at the Corner of Bitter and Sweet* +	high school	novel
Fountain, Ben	*Billy Lynn's Long Halftime Walk*	high school	novel
Fuller, Claire	*Our Endless Numbered Days* +	high school	novel
Gaiman, Neil	*American Gods*	high school	novel
Gaiman, Neil	*Neverwhere* +	high school	novel
Ghosh, Amitav	*Sea of Poppies*	high school	novel
Gordimer, Nadine	*The Pickup*	high school	novel
Grossman, David	*Someone to Run With*	high school	novel
Guene, Faiza	*Kiffe Kiffe Tomorrow* +	high school	novel
Haddon, Mark	*Curious Incident of the Dog in the Night-Time* +	high school	novel
Hamid, Mohsin	*Exit West*	high school	novel

AUTHOR	TITLE	LEVEL	GENRE
Hamid, Mohsin	*The Reluctant Fundamentalist*	high school	novel
Harkaway, Nick	*Tigerman*	high school	novel
Hemon, Aleksandar	*The Lazarus Project*	high school	novel
Hosseini, Khaled	*A Thousand Splendid Suns*	high school	novel
Ishiguru, Kazuo	*Never Let Me Go*	high school	novel
Johnson, Adam	*The Orphan Master's Son*	high school	novel
Jones, Lloyd	*Mister Pip*	high school	novel
Joyce, Rachel	*The Unlikely Pilgrimage of Harold Fry*	high school	novel
Kang, Han	*The Vegetarian*	high school	novel
Koch, Herman	*The Dinner*	high school	novel
Kushner, Rachel	*Telex from Cuba*	high school	novel
Kushner, Rachel	*The Flamethrowers*	high school	novel
Lahiri, Jhumpa	*The Lowland*	high school	novel
Lalami, Laila	*Hope and Other Dangerous Pursuits*	high school	novel
Larsson, Stieg	*Girl with the Dragon Tattoo*	high school	novel
Lee, Chang-rae	*On Such a Full Sea*	high school	novel
LeGuin, Ursula	*The Left Hand of Darkness*	high school	novel
Lerner, Ben	*10:04*	high school	novel
Lerner, Ben	*Leaving the Atocha Station*	high school	novel
Lessing, Doris	*The Fifth Child*	high school	novel
Lethem, Jonathan	*Chronic City*	high school	novel
Lewycka, Marina	*A Short History of Tractors in Ukrainian*	high school	novel
Livaneli, O. Z.	*Bliss*	high school	novel
Locke, Attica	*Black Water Rising*	high school	novel
Magoon, Kekla	*How It Went Down +*	high school	novel
Mahjan, Karan	*The Association of Small Bombs*	high school	novel
Malkani, Gautam	*Londonstani*	high school	novel

AUTHOR	TITLE	LEVEL	GENRE
Márquez, Gabriel García	*Chronicle of a Death Foretold*	high school	novel
Marra, Anthony	*A Constellation of Vital Phenomena*	high school	novel
Martin, George R. R.	*Game of Thrones*	high school	novel
McBride, James	*The Good Lord Bird*	high school	novel
McCann, Colum	*Let the Great World Spin*	high school	novel
McCarthy, Cormac	*The Road*	high school	novel
McCormick, Patricia	*Cut*	high school	novel
McCormick, Patricia	*Sold*	high school	novel
McEwan, Ian	*On Chesil Beach*	high school	novel
McGuire, Ian	*The North Water*	high school	novel
Menedez, Ana	*Loving Che*	high school	novel
Mengestu, Dinaw	*All Our Names*	high school	novel
Mengestu, Dinaw	*How to Read the Air*	high school	novel
Messud, Claire	*The Emperor's Children*	high school	novel
Mieville, China	*The City the City*	high school	novel
Mitchell, David	*Black Swan Green*	high school	novel
Mitchell, David	*Cloud Atlas*	high school	novel
Mitchell, David	*The Bone Clocks*	high school	novel
Mitchell, David	*The Thousand Autumns of Jacob de Zoet*	high school	novel
Montero, Mayra	*Dancing to Almendra*	high school	novel
Morrison, Toni	*A Mercy*	high school	novel
Morrison, Toni	*Home*	high school	novel
Mosley, Walter	*The Last Days of Ptolemy Grey*	high school	novel
Müller, Herta	*The Hunger Angel*	high school	novel
Müller, Herta	*The Land of Green Plums*	high school	novel
Müller, Herta	*The Passport*	high school	novel

AUTHOR	TITLE	LEVEL	GENRE
Murakami, Haruki	*After Dark*	high school	novel
Murakami, Haruki	*Colorless Tsukuru Tazaki and His Years of Pilgrimage*	high school	novel
Ndiaye, Marie	*Ladivine*	high school	novel
Ndiaye, Marie	*Three Strong Women*	high school	novel
Nguyen, Viet Thanh	*The Sympathizer*	high school	novel
Nothomb, Amelie	*The Character of Rain* +	high school	novel
O'Nan, Stewart	*Last Night at the Lobster*	high school	novel
O'Neill, Joseph	*Netherland*	high school	novel
Obreht, Tea	*The Tiger's Wife*	high school	novel
Oeyemi, Helen	*The Icarus Girl*	high school	novel
Ogawa, Koko	*The Housekeeper and the Professor* +	high school	novel
Ondaatje, Michael	*Divisadero*	high school	novel
Ondaatje, Michael	*The Cat's Table*	high school	novel
Otsuka, Julie	*The Buddha in the Attic*	high school	novel
Oz, Amos	*My Michael*	high school	novel
Oz, Amos	*Scenes from Village Life*	high school	novel
Pamuk, Orhan	*My Name Is Red*	high school	novel
Pamuk, Orhan	*Snow*	high school	novel
Pessl, Marisha	*Special Topics in Calamity Physics*	high school	novel
Petterson, Per	*Out Stealing Horses*	high school	novel
Powell, William Campbell	*Expiration Day* +	high school	novel
Powers, Kevin	*The Yellow Birds*	high school	novel
Powers, Richard	*The Echo Maker*	high school	novel
Price, Richard	*Lush Life*	high school	novel
Prose, Francine	*Mister Monkey*	high school	novel

AUTHOR	TITLE	LEVEL	GENRE
Rahman, Zia Haider	*In the Light of What We Know*	high school	novel
Rash, Ron	*Serena*	high school	novel
Robinson, Marilynne	*Home*	high school	novel
Robinson, Marilynne	*Lila*	high school	novel
Rushdie, Salman	*Haroun and the Sea of Stories*	high school	novel
Saramago, José	*Blindness*	high school	novel
Saramago, José	*Seeing*	high school	novel
Sebald, W. B.	*Austerlitz*	high school	novel
Shaffer, Mary Ann, and Annie Barrows	*The Guernsey Literary and Potato Peel Pie Society*	high school	novel
Shriver, Lionel	*We Need to Talk About Kevin*	high school	novel
Shteyngart, Gary	*Super Sad Love Story*	high school	novel
Sinha, Indra	*Animal's People*	high school	novel
Skloot, Rebecca	*The Immortal Life of Henrietta Lacks*	high school	novel
Smith, Zadie	*NW*	high school	novel
Smith, Zadie	*On Beauty*	high school	novel
Smith, Zadie	*Swing Time*	high school	novel
Spufford, Francis	*Golden Hill*	high school	novel
Szalay, David	*All That Man Is*	high school	novel
Tartt, Donna	*The Goldfinch*	high school	novel
Thomas, Angie	*The Hate U Give*	high school	novel
Torres, Justin	*We, the Animals*	high school	novel
Tremain, Rose	*The Gustav Sonata*	high school	novel
Verghese, Abraham	*Cutting for Stone*	high school	novel
Weir, Andy	*The Martian*	high school	novel
Whitehead, Colson	*The Underground Railroad*	high school	novel
Wiggins, Marianne	*The Shadow Catcher*	high school	novel

AUTHOR	TITLE	LEVEL	GENRE
Williams, John	*Stoner*	high school	novel
Woodson, Jacqueline	*Another Brooklyn*	high school	novel
Wroblewski, David	*The Story of Edgar Sawtelle*	high school	novel
Yehoshua, A. B.	*A Woman in Jerusalem*	high school	novel
Cruz, Nilo	*Anna in the Tropics*	high school	play
Letts, Tracy	*August: Osage County*	high school	play
Reza, Yasmina	*Art*	high school	play
Finney, Nikki	*Head Off and Split: Poems*	high school	poetry
Rankine, Claudia	*Citizen: An American Lyric*	high school	poetry
Szymborska, Wisława	*Map*	high school	poetry
Adichie, Chimamanda Ngozi	*The Thing Around Your Neck*	high school	short stories
Aleichem, Sholem	*Tevye the Dairyman and Motl the Cantor's Son*	high school	short stories
Calvino, Italo	*Invisible Cities*	high school	short stories
Campbell, Bobbie Jo	*American Salvage*	high school	short stories
Davis, Lydia	*Can't and Won't: Stories*	high school	short stories
Díaz, Junot	*This Is How You Lose Her*	high school	short stories
Keret, Etgar	*The Bus Driver Who Wanted to Be God*	high school	short stories
Klay, Phil	*Redeployment*	high school	short stories
Lahiri, Jhumpa	*Unaccustomed Earth*	high school	short stories
Li, Yiyun	*Gold Boy, Emerald Girl*	high school	short stories
Marra, Anthony	*The Tsar of Love and Techno*	high school	short stories
Mueenuddin, Daniyal	*In Other Rooms, Other Wonders*	high school	short stories
Nguyen, Viet Thanh	*The Refugees*	high school	short stories
Ozick, Cynthia	*Dictation: A Quartet*	high school	short stories
Ozick, Cynthia	*The Shawl*	high school	short stories
Sanders, George	*The Tenth of December*	high school	short stories

AUTHOR	TITLE	LEVEL	GENRE
Anderson, M. T.	*Symphony for the City of the Dead: Dmitry Shostokovich and the Leningrad Symphony* *	middle school	biography
Fleming, Candace	*Amelia Lost*	middle school	biography
Freedman, Russell	*Eleanor Roosevelt*	middle school	biography
Greenberg, Jan, and Sandra Jordan	*Vincent Van Gogh: Portrait of an Artist*	middle school	biography
Heiligman, Deborah	*Charles and Emma: The Darwins' Leap of Faith*	middle school	biography
Herrera, Juan Felipe	*Portraits of Hispanic American Heroes*	middle school	biography
Kidder, Tracy	*Mountains Beyond Mountains: Adapted for Young People*	middle school	biography
Kurlansky, Mark	*Frozen in Time: Clarence Birdseye's Outrageous Idea*	middle school	biography
Nelson, Vaunda Micheaux	*No Crystal Stair: Life of Lewis Michaux, Harlem Bookseller*	middle school	biography
Sheinkin, Steve	*The Notorious Benedict Arnold*	middle school	biography
Silvey, Anita	*Let Your Voice Be Heard: The Life and Times of Pete Seeger*	middle school	biography
Sweet, Melissa	*Some Writer! The Story of E. B. White*	middle school	biography
Turner, Pamela	*Samurai Rising: The Epic Life of Minamoto Yoshitsune*	middle school	biography
Nelson, Marilyn	*Carver: A Life in Poems*	middle school	biography in verse
Gratz, Alan	*Refugee*	middle school	fiction
Ottaviani, Jim, and Maris Wicks	*Primates: The Fearless Science of Jane Goodall, Dian Fossey, and Biruté Galdikas*	middle school	graphic biography
Satrapi, Marjane	*Persepolis: The Story of a Childhood* *	middle school	graphic memoir
Satrapi, Marjane	*Persepolis 2: The Story of a Return* *	middle school	graphic memoir
Brown, Don	*Drowned City: Hurricane Katrina and New Orleans* *	middle school	graphic nonfiction

AUTHOR	TITLE	LEVEL	GENRE
Brown, Don	*The Great American Dust Bowl*	middle school	graphic nonfiction
Pullman, Philip, and Fred Fordham	*The Adventures of John Blake: Mystery of the Ghost Ship*	middle school	graphic novel
Wiesner, David, and Donna Jo Napoli	*Fish Girl*	middle school	graphic novel
Yang, Gene Luen	*American Born Chinese*	middle school	graphic novel
Yang, Gene Luen, and Thien Pham	*Level Up*	middle school	graphic novel
Anderson, Laurie Halse	*Chains*	middle school	historical fiction
Bruchac, Joseph	*The Winter People*	middle school	historical fiction
Carbone, Elisa	*Blood on the River*	middle school	historical fiction
Rhodes, Jewell Parker	*Towers Falling*	middle school	historical fiction
Ryan, Pam Muñoz	*Echo*	middle school	historical fiction
Shabazz, Ilyasah, and Kekla Magoon	*X: A Novel*	middle school	historical fiction
Winthrop, Elizabeth	*Counting on Grace*	middle school	historical fiction
Barakat, Ibtisam	*Tasting the Sky: A Palestinian Childhood* *	middle school	memoir
Goodall, Jane	*My Life with the Chimpanzees*	middle school	memoir
Jiménez, Francisco	*Breaking Through*	middle school	memoir
Jiménez, Francisco	*The Circuit*	middle school	memoir
Kristofic, Jim	*Navajos Wear Nikes: A Reservation Life*	middle school	memoir
Meyers, Walter Dean	*Bad Boy: A Memoir*	middle school	memoir
Rusesabagina, Paul	*An Ordinary Man: An Autobiography*	middle school	memoir
Engle, Margarita	*Enchanted Air: Two Cultures, Two Wings*	middle school	memoir in verse

AUTHOR	TITLE	LEVEL	GENRE
Woodson, Jacqueline	*Brown Girl Dreaming*	middle school	memoir in verse
Gaiman, Neil	*Norse Mythology*	middle school	mythology
Riordan, Rick	*Percy Jackson's Greek Gods*	middle school	mythology
Rylant, Cynthia	*The Beautiful Stories of Life*	middle school	mythology
Alexander, Kwame	*The Playbook*	middle school	nonfiction
Aronson, Marc	*Sugar Changed the World*	middle school	nonfiction
Aronson, Marc	*Trapped: How the World Rescued 33 Miners*	middle school	nonfiction
Bartoletti, Susan Campbell	*Hitler Youth*	middle school	nonfiction
Bartoletti, Susan Campbell	*Terrible Typhoid Mary: A True Story of the Deadliest Cook in America*	middle school	nonfiction
Bascomb, Neal	*The Nazi Hunters* *	middle school	nonfiction
Blumenthal, Karen	*Tommy: The Gun That Changed America*	middle school	nonfiction
Bolden, Tonya	*Searching for Sarah Rector: The Richest Black Girl in America*	middle school	nonfiction
Brimner, Larry Dane	*Strike! The Farm Workers' Fight for Their Rights*	middle school	nonfiction
Brimner, Larry Dane	*The Rain Wizard*	middle school	nonfiction
Brown, Daniel James	*The Boys in the Boat: The True Story of an American Team's Epic Journey to Win Gold at the 1936 Olympics (young readers adaptation)*	middle school	nonfiction
Castaldo, Nancy	*Beastly Brains*	middle school	nonfiction
Castaldo, Nancy	*The Story of Seeds*	middle school	nonfiction
Castaldo, Nancy	*Seeds*	middle school	nonfiction
Cherrix, Amy	*Eye of the Storm*	middle school	nonfiction
Fleischman, Paul	*Eyes Wide Open* *	middle school	nonfiction
Fleming, Candace	*The Family Romanov*	middle school	nonfiction
Freedman, Russell	*Angel Island*	middle school	nonfiction

AUTHOR	TITLE	LEVEL	GENRE
Freedman, Russell	*Freedom Walkers*	middle school	nonfiction
Freedman, Russell	*Kids at Work: Lewis Hine and the Crusade Against Child Labor*	middle school	nonfiction
Freedman, Russell	*We Will Not Be Silent*	middle school	nonfiction
Frydenborg, Kay	*A Dog in the Cave*	middle school	nonfiction
Goodall, Jane	*Jane Goodall: 50 Years at Gombe*	middle school	nonfiction
Hari, Daoud	*The Translator*	middle school	nonfiction
Hellingman, Deborah	*Vincent and Theo: The Van Gogh Brothers*	middle school	nonfiction
Hoose, Phillip	*Moonbird*	middle school	nonfiction
Hoose, Phillip	*The Boys Who Challenged Hitler*	middle school	nonfiction
Jarrow, Gail	*Bubonic Panic*	middle school	nonfiction
Jarrow, Gail	*Fatal Fever: Tracking Down Typhoid Mary*	middle school	nonfiction
Leahy, Stephen	*Your Water Footprint*	middle school	nonfiction
Levinson, Cynthia	*We've Got a Job*	middle school	nonfiction
Marrin, Albert	*Black Gold: The Story of Oil in Our Lives*	middle school	nonfiction
Marrin, Albert	*Flesh and Blood So Cheap: The Triangle Fire and Its Legacy*	middle school	nonfiction
McCormick, Patricia	*The Plot to Kill Hitler: Dietrich Bonhoeffer* *	middle school	nonfiction
McKissack, Patricia	*Black Hands, White Sails*	middle school	nonfiction
Montgomery, Sy	*Amazon Adventure*	middle school	nonfiction
Murphy, Jim	*An American Plague*	middle school	nonfiction
Murphy, Jim	*The Great Fire*	middle school	nonfiction
Nazario, Sonia	*Enrique's Journey* *	middle school	nonfiction
Oppenheim, Joanne	*Dear Miss Breed*	middle school	nonfiction
Plain, Nancy	*This Strange Wilderness: The Life and Art of John James Audubon*	middle school	nonfiction

AUTHOR	TITLE	LEVEL	GENRE
Pollan, Michael	*The Omnivore's Dilemma: The Secrets Behind What You Eat (young readers edition)*	middle school	nonfiction
Schlosser, Eric, and Charles Wilson	*Chew on This*	middle school	nonfiction
Sheinkin, Steve	*Most Dangerous: Daniel Ellsberg and the Secret History of the Vietnam War* *	middle school	nonfiction
Sheinkin, Steve	*The Port Chicago 50: Disaster, Mutiny, and the Fight for Civil Rights*	middle school	nonfiction
Sheinkin, Steve	*Bomb: The Race to Build (and Steal) the World's Most Dangerous Weapon*	middle school	nonfiction
Sheinkin, Steve	*Undefeated: Jim Thorpe and the Carlisle Indian School Football Team* *	middle school	nonfiction
Shetterly, Margot Lee	*Hidden Figures (young readers' edition)* *	middle school	nonfiction
Stelson, Caren	*Sachiko: A Nagasaki Bomb Survivor's Story*	middle school	nonfiction
Swanson, James L.	*Chasing Lincoln's Killer*	middle school	nonfiction
Swanson, James L.	*The President Has Been Shot*	middle school	nonfiction
Hoose, Phillip	*Claudette Colvin: Twice Toward Justice*	middle school	nonfiction
Adam Gidwitz	*The Inquisitor's Tale*	middle school	novel
Agosin, Marjorie	*I Lived on Butterfly Hill*	middle school	novel
Anderson, Laurie Halse	*The Impossible Knife of Memory*	middle school	novel
Angleberger, Tom	*Fuzzy*	middle school	novel
Applegate, Katherine	*Crenshaw*	middle school	novel
Aveyard, Victoria	*Red Queen* *	middle school	novel
Barnhill, Kelly	*The Girl Who Drank the Moon*	middle school	novel
Bernal, Estela	*Can You See Me Now?*	middle school	novel
Block, Francesca Lia	*Love in the Time of Global Warming* *	middle school	novel
Bradley, Kimberly Brubaker	*The War That Saved My Life*	middle school	novel

AUTHOR	TITLE	LEVEL	GENRE
Card, Orson Scott	*Ender's Game* *	middle school	novel
Collins, Suzanne	*The Hunger Games*	middle school	novel
Crowder, Melanie	*Parched*	middle school	novel
DiCamillo, Kate	*The Magician's Elephant*	middle school	novel
Dicks, Matthew	*Memoirs of an Imaginary Friend* *	middle school	novel
Draper, Sharon	*Out of My Mind* *	middle school	novel
Dumas, Firoozeh	*It Ain't So Awful, Falafel*	middle school	novel
Dunn, Mark	*Ella Minnow Pea*	middle school	novel
Ellis, Deborah	*The Breadwinner*	middle school	novel
Erdrich, Louise	*Chickadee*	middle school	novel
Erskine, Kathryn	*Mockingbird*	middle school	novel
Gaiman, Neil	*The Graveyard Book*	middle school	novel
Gaiman, Neil	*The Ocean at the End of the Lane*	middle school	novel
Gantos, Jeff	*Dead End in Norvelt*	middle school	novel
Hornby, Nick	*Slam*	middle school	novel
Johnson, Angela	*The First Part Last* *	middle school	novel
Kadohata, Cynthia	*Kira-Kira*	middle school	novel
Lackhart, E.	*We Were Liars*	middle school	novel
LaValley, Josanne	*Factory Girl*	middle school	novel
Lin, Grace	*Where the Mountain Meets the Moon*	middle school	novel
Lloyd, Natalie	*A Snicker of Magic*	middle school	novel
Miller, Kirsten	*Kiki Strike: Inside the Shadow City*	middle school	novel
Morpurgo, Michael	*Private Peaceful* *	middle school	novel
Morpurgo, Michael	*The Elephant in the Garden*	middle school	novel
Moss, Miriam	*Girl on a Plane*	middle school	novel
Na, An	*A Step from Heaven*	middle school	novel
Ness, Patrick	*A Monster Calls*	middle school	novel

AUTHOR	TITLE	LEVEL	GENRE
Palacio, R. J.	*Wonder* *	middle school	novel
Park, Linda Sue	*A Long Walk to Water*	middle school	novel
Park, Linda Sue	*A Single Shard*	middle school	novel
Patterson, James	*Maximum Ride*	middle school	novel
Pennypacker, Sarah	*Pax*	middle school	novel
Philbrick, Rodman	*Zane and the Hurricane: A Story of Katrina*	middle school	novel
Reynolds, Jason	*Miles Morales: Spider-Man*	middle school	novel
Reynolds, Jason	*A Long Way Down*	middle school	novel
Reynolds, Jason, and Brendan Kiely	*All American Boys* *	middle school	novel
Rorby, Ginny	*How to Speak Dolphin*	middle school	novel
Roth, Veronica	*Divergent* *	middle school	novel
Ruby, Laura	*Bone Gap*	middle school	novel
Rushdie, Salman	*Luka and the Fire of Life*	middle school	novel
Sáenz, Benjamin Alire	*The Inexplicable Logic of My Life* *	middle school	novel
Sáenz, Benjamin Alire	*Aristotle and Dante Discover the Secrets of the Universe* *	middle school	novel
Saunders, Kate	*Five Children on the Western Front*	middle school	novel
Schmitt, Eric-Emmanuell	*Monsieur Ibrahim and the Flowers of the Koran* *	middle school	novel
Schrefer, Eliot	*Endangered*	middle school	novel
Schrefer, Eliot	*Threatened*	middle school	novel
Sepetys, Ruta	*Salt to the Sea* *	middle school	novel
Shusterman, Neal	*Challenger Deep*	middle school	novel
Stork, Francisco X.	*Marcelo in the Real World*	middle school	novel
Ursu, Anne	*The Real Boy*	middle school	novel
Vaught, Susan	*Things Too Huge to Fix*	middle school	novel

AUTHOR	TITLE	LEVEL	GENRE
Vizzini, Ned	*Be More Cool* *	middle school	novel
Watson, Renee	*Piecing Me Together* *	middle school	novel
Williams-Garcia, Rita	*Clayton Byrd Goes Underground*	middle school	novel
Wilson, N. D.	*Boys of Blur*	middle school	novel
Zusak, Markus	*The Book Thief* *	middle school	novel
Alexander, Kwame	*Booked*	middle school	novel in verse
Alexander, Kwame	*Solo* *	middle school	novel in verse
Alexander, Kwame	*The Crossover*	middle school	novel in verse
Crossan, Sarah	*One*	middle school	novel in verse
Crowder, Melanie	*Audacity*	middle school	novel in verse
Engle, Margarita	*Forest World*	middle school	novel in verse
Engle, Margarita	*The Wild Book*	middle school	novel in verse
Lai, Thanhha	*Inside Out and Back Again*	middle school	novel in verse
Nelson, Marilyn	*American Ace*	middle school	novel in verse
Lester, Julius	*Day of Tears*	middle school	play
Meyers, Walter Dean	*Riot* *	middle school	play
Grimes, Nikki	*One Last Word* *	middle school	poetry
Herrera, Juan Felipe	*Laughing Out Loud, I Fly*	middle school	poetry
Nye, Naomi Shihab	*The Flag of Childhood: Poems from the Middle East* *	middle school	poetry
Park, Linda Sue	*Tap Dancing on the Roof: Sijo*	middle school	poetry
Nelson, Marilyn	*My Seneca Village* *	middle school	poetry

Appendix C

Recommendations from Avid Readers

10 Books That Took Me Places I Had Never Been but Needed to Go

1. *Golden Hill: A Novel of Old New York*, Francis Spufford

2. *Pachinko*, Min Jin Lee

3. *The Bone Readers*, Jacob Ross

4. *The God of Love and Techno*, Anthony Marra

5. *The Golden Legend*, Nadeem Aslam

6. *Judas*, Amos Oz

7. *A Horse Walks into a Bar*, David Grossman

8. *Selection Day*, Aravind Adiga

9. *Waking Lions*, Ayelet Gundar-Goshen

10. *Salt Houses*, Hala Alyan

10 Books Full of Dark Truths
That Offer Hope in the Unseen

1. *The Blood of Emmett Till*, Timothy Tyson

2. *Stamped from the Beginning: The Definitive History of Racist Ideas in America*, Ibram X. Kendi

3. *The Optician of Lampedusa*, Emma Jane Kirby

4. *Exodus: How Migration Is Changing the World*, Paul Collier

5. *Hope in the Dark: Untold Histories, Wild Possibilities*, Rebecca Solnit

6. *Tears We Cannot Stop: A Sermon to White America*, Michael Eric Dyson

7. *Evicted: Poverty and Profit in the American City*, Matthew Desmond

8. *East West Street: On the Origins of Genocide and Crimes Against America*, Phillippe Sands

9. *Blood at the Root: A Racial Cleansing in America*, Patrick Phillips

10. *The Fire This Time: A New Generation Speaks About Race*, Jesmyn Ward

10 Memoirs That Enlarged My Life

1. *You Don't Have to Say You Love Me*, Sherman Alexie

2. *Dare to Disappoint: Growing Up in Turkey*, Ozge Samanci

3. *Fun Home: A Family Tragicomic*, Alison Bechdel

4. *Hunger: A Memoir of (My) Body*, Roxane Gay

5. *The Distance Between Us*, Reyna Grande

6. *Born a Crime: Stories from a South African Childhood*, Trevor Noah

7. *Barbarian Days: A Surfing Life*, William Finnegan

8. *Hillbilly Elegy: A Memoir of a Family and Culture in Crisis*, J. D. Vance

9. *When Breath Becomes Air*, Paul Kalanithi

10. *The Light of the World*, Elizabeth Alexander

10 Books for Ten-Year-Old Boys Who Want Something They Cannot Put Down

Recommended by Brennan Kajder (age 10)

1. *The One and Only Ivan*, Katherine Applegate

2. *Ghost*, Jason Reynolds

3. *The Hazardous Tales* series (especially *Treaties, Trenches, Mud,* and *Blood*), Nathan Hale

4. *The Magnus Chase and the Gods of Asgard* series, Rick Riordan

5. *Harry Potter and the Philosopher's Stone* (because the UK version sounds better in your head), J. K. Rowling

6. *The Wings of Fire* series, Tui Sutherland

7. *The Amulet* series (graphic novels make you think, too), Kazu Kibuishi

8. *Five Kingdoms*, Brandon Mull

9. *The False Prince*, Jennifer Nielsen

10. *Imaginary Veterinary*, Suzanne Selfors

10 Adventure Books for Twelve-Year-Old Boys

Recommended by Matthew Kajder (age 12)

1. *The Iron Trial* series, Cassandra Clare and Holly Black

2. *The Unwanteds* series, Lisa McMann

3. *The False Prince*, Jennifer Nielsen

4. *The How to Train Your Dragon* series, Cressida Crowell

5. *Lost Stars*, Claudia Gray

6. *The Masterminds* series, Gordan Korman

7. *The Lightning Thief*, Rick Riordan

8. *MiNRS*, Kevin Sylvester

9. *Hatchet*, Gary Paulsen

10. *The Missing* series, Margaret Peterson Haddix

10 Books for Teens Who Don't Know Much About History but Would Like To

By Will Fitzhugh, editor of the *Concord Review*

1. *Mornings on Horseback*, David McCullough

2. *Washington's Crossing*, David Hackett Fischer

3. *Battle Cry of Freedom*, James McPherson

4. *The Path Between the Seas*, David McCullough

5. *Miracle at Philadelphia*, Katherine Drinker Bowen

6. *Stalingrad*, Antony Beevor

7. *Endurance*, Alfred Lansing

8. *Miss Leavitt's Stars*, George Johnson

9. *Longitude*, Dava Sobel

10. *Alexander Hamilton*, Ron Chernow

10 Books I Believe Should Be Taught
in High School

1. *The Mersault Investigations*, Kamil Daod

2. *Behind the Beautiful Forevers*, Katherine Boo

3. *The Good Soldiers*, David Finkel

4. *The Sixth Extinction*, Elizabeth Kolbert

5. *The Crusades of Cesar Chavez: A Biography*, Miriam Pawel

6. *Lila*, Marilyn Robinson

7. *East West*, Mohsin Hamid

8. *Between the World and Me*, Ta-Nehisi Coates

9. *March* trilogy, John Lewis, Andrew Adin, and Nate Powell

10. *All ten plays of August Wilson*

10 Must-Have Books of Poetry

1. *Every Riven Thing*, Christian Wiman

2. *1914: Poetry Remembers*, edited by Carol Ann Duffy

3. *The Essential Gwendolyn Brooks*, Gwendolyn Brooks

4. *Citizen: An American Lyric*, Claudia Rankine

5. *Head Off and Split*, Nikki Finney

6. *My Seneca Village*, Marilyn Nelson

7. *The Best of It*, Kay Ryan

8. *Aimless Love*, Billy Collins

9. *Life on Mars*, Tracy K. Smith

10. *Lighthead*, Terrance Hayes

10 Recommendations for Your
Next Book-Club Meeting

1. *An Unnecessary Woman*, Rabih Allamedine

2. *The Sellout*, Paul Beatty

3. *A Little Life*, Hanya Yanagihara

4. *The Overstory,* Richard Powers

5. *Snow*, Orham Pamuk

6. *The North Water*, Ian McGuire

7. *Zero K*, Don Delillo

8. *LaRose*, Louise Erdrich

9. *The Noise of Time*, Julian Barnes

10. *The Underground Railroad*, Colson Whitehead

Works Cited

ACT. 2017. *Preparing for the ACT Test: 2016–2017*. Iowa City, IA: ACT. www.act.org /content/dam/act/unsecured/documents/Preparing-for-the-ACT.pdf.

Adams, M. 2010–11. "Advancing Our Students' Language and Literacy: The Challenge of Complex Texts." *American Educator* 34 (4): 3–11, 53.

Alexander, Elizabeth. 2016. *The Light of the World: A Memoir*. New York: Grand Central Books.

Alexander, Kwame. 2014. *The Crossover*. Boston: HMH.

Alexander, Michelle. 2012. *The New Jim Crow: Mass Incarceration in the Age of Color-blindness*. New York: New Press.

Anderson, Laurie Halse. 2011. *Fever 1793*. New York: Atheneum Books.

Applebee, Arthur N. 1989. *A Study of Book-Length Works Taught in High School English Programs*. Report Series 1.2. Albany, NY: Center for the Learning and Teaching of Literature.

Atwell, Nancie, and Ann Atwell Merkel. 2016. *The Reading Zone: How to Help Kids Become Skilled, Passionate, Habitual, Critical Readers*. 2d edition. New York: Scholastic Professional.

Atwood, Margaret. 2004. *Oryx and Crake*. New York: Anchor.

———. 2010. *The Year of the Flood*. New York: Anchor.

Baldwin, James. 1992. *The Fire Next Time*. New York: Vintage.

Barry, Mary Nguyen, and Michael Dannenberg. 2016. *Out of Pocket: The High Cost of Inadequate High Schools and High School Student Achievement on College Affordability*. Washington, DC, and New York: Education Reform Now.

Bartoletti, Susan Campbell. 2015. *Terrible Typhoid Mary: The True Story of the Deadliest Cook in America*. Boston: HMH.

Bascomb, Neal. 2009. *Hunting Eichman: How a Band of Survivors and a Young Spy Agency Chased Down the World's Most Notorious Nazi*. Boston: Mariner Books.

———. 2013. *The Nazi Hunters: How a Team of Spies and Survivors Captured the World's Most Notorious Nazi*. New York: Arthur A. Levine Books.

Beck, Isabel L., Margaret G. McKeown, and Linda Kucan. 2002. *Bringing Words to Life: Robust Vocabulary Instruction.* New York: Guilford.

Block, Francesca Lia. 2004. *Weetzie Bat.* New York: HarperCollins.

Bloom, Harold. 2011. *The Anatomy of Influence: Literature as a Way of Life.* New Haven, CT: Yale University Press.

Boo, Katherine. 2014. *Behind the Beautiful Forevers: Life, Death, and Hope in a Mumbai Undercity.* New York: Random House.

Brontë, Emily. 2010. *Wuthering Heights.* New York: William Collins.

Brown, Don 2013. *The Great American Dust Bowl.* Boston: HMH.

Cain, Sian. 2017. "Ebook sales continue to fall as younger generations drive appetite for print." March 14. *The Guardian.* www.theguardian.com/books/2017/mar/14/ebook-sales-continue-to-fall-nielsen-survey-uk-book-sales.

Castaldo, Nancy F. 2016. *The Story of Seeds: From Mendel's Garden to Your Plate, and How There's More of Less to Eat Around the World.* Boston: HMH.

Cherrix, Amy. 2017. *Eye of the Storm: NASA, Drones, and the Race to Crack the Hurricane Code.* Boston: HMH.

Chopin, Kate. 1993. *The Awakening.* New York: W.W. Norton.

Clinton, Catherine. 2017. *I, Too, Sing America: Three Centuries of African American Poetry.* Boston: HMH.

Coates, Ta-Nehisi. 2015. *Between the World and Me.* New York: Spiegel and Grau.

Coetzee, J. M. 2017. *Disgrace: A Novel.* New York: Penguin.

Conrad, Joseph. 2006. *Heart of Darkness.* Project Gutenberg. www.gutenberg.org/cache/epub/526/pg526-images.html.

Cullen, Countee. 2013. *Countee Cullen: Collected Poems.* New York: Library of America.

Daoud, Kamil. 2015. *The Mersault Investigation.* New York: Other Press.

Desmond, Matthew. 2017. *Evicted: Poverty and Profit in an American City.* New York: Broadway Books.

Dickens, Charles. 2010. *A Tale of Two Cities.* E-book. Public domain.

Dickinson, Emily. 2013. *The Complete Poems of Emily Dickinson*. E-book. Heraklion Press.

Doerr, Anthony. 2017. *All the Light We Cannot See*. New York: Scribner.

Duckworth, Angela. 2016. *Grit: The Power and Passion of Perseverance*. New York: Scribner.

Dweck, Carole. 2007. *Mindset: The New Psychology of Success*. New York: Ballentine Books.

Eco, Umberto. 1994. *Six Walks in the Fictional Woods*. Cambridge, MA: Harvard University Press.

Erdrich, Louise. 2013. *The Round House*. New York: Harper.

Eren, A. Murat. 2017. "Candidate Phyla Radiation in Human Blood?" *Meren Lab Blog*, August 23. http://merenlab.org/2017/08/23/CPR-in-blood/.

Farrington, Camille A., Melissa Roderick, Elaine Allensworth, Jenny Nagaoka, Tasha Seneca Keyes, David W. Johnson, and Nicole O. Beechum. 2012. *Teaching Adolescents to Become Learners: The Role of Noncognitive Factors in Shaping School Performance: A Critical Literature Review*. Chicago: University of Chicago Consortium on Chicago School Research.

Faulkner, William. 1990a. *Absalom, Absalom!* New York: Vintage.

———. 1990b. *The Sound and the Fury*. New York: Vintage.

Finkel, David. 2010. *The Good Soldiers*. New York: Picador.

Fountain, Ben. 2016. *Billy Lynn's Long Halftime Walk*. New York: Ecco.

Freedman, Russell. 1998. *Kids at Work: Lewis Hine and the Crusade Against Child Labor*. Boston: HMH.

———. 2016. *We Will Not Be Silent: The White Rose Student Resistance Movement That Defied Hitler*. Boston: Clarion Books.

Frost, Robert. 2002. *The Poetry of Robert Frost: The Collected Poems*. New York: Holt.

Gaiman, Neal. 2007. *M Is for Magic*. New York: HarperTrophy. www.8novels.net /fiction/u3067.html.

———. 2012. *Coraline*. New York: HarperCollins.

———. 2015. *Neverwhere*. New York: William Morrow.

Gárcia Márquez, Gabriel. 2008. *Collected Stories*. New York: Harper Perennial Modern Classics.

Gárcia Márquez, Gabriel. 1982. "The Solitude of Latin America." Nobel Lecture, Stockholm, Sweden, December 8. Available at www.nobelprize.org/nobel _prizes/literature/laureates/1982/marquez-lecture.html.

Gilson, D. 2017. "Where the Wild Things Go." *Poetry* (May).

Graff, Gerald, and Cathy Birkenstein. 2014. *"They Say / I Say": The Moves That Matter in Academic Writing*. 3d edition. New York: W. W. Norton.

Grahame, Kenneth. 1908. *The Wind in the Willows*. New York: Charles Scribner's Sons. Available online at www.online-literature.com/grahame/windwillows/1/.

Grande, Reyna. 2016. *The Distance Between Us*. Young Readers Edition. New York: Aladdin.

Green, John. 2008. *Looking for Alaska*. New York: Speak.

———. 2012. *The Fault in Our Stars*. New York: Speak.

Guinness World Records. 2017. *Guinness World Records 2017*. New York: GWR.

Gutterson, David. 1995. *Snow Falling on Cedars*. New York: Vintage.

Hamid, Mohsin. 2017. *Exit West*. New York: Riverhead Books.

Harris, Robert. 2017. *Conclave*. New York: Vintage.

Hawthorne, Nathaniel. 2015. *The Scarlet Letter*. Ballingslöv, Sweden: Wisehouse Classics.

Hersey, John. 1989. *Hiroshima*. New York: Vintage.

Honig, Bill, Linda Diamond, Linda Gutlohn, and Jacalyn Mahler. 2000. *Teaching Reading Sourcebook: For Kindergarten Through Eighth Grade*. Novato, CA: Academic Therapy.

Hoose, Phillip. 2015. *The Boys Who Challenged Hitler: Knud Pederson and the Churchill Club*. New York: Farrar, Straus and Giroux.

Housman, A. E. 1896. *A Shropshire Lad*. London: K. Paul, Trench, Treubner.

Hurston, Zora Neal. 2000. *Their Eyes Were Watching God*. New York: Harper.

Ishiguro, Kazuo. 2006. *Never Let Me Go*. New York: Vintage.

Jackson, C. Kirabo. 2014. *Non-Cognitive Ability, Test Scores, and Teacher Quality: Evidence from 9th Grade Teachers in North Carolina*. NBER Working Paper No. 18624. Originally issued 2012. Cambridge, MA: National Bureau of Economic Research.

Jago, Carol. 1999. *Nikki Giovanni in the Classroom: The Same Ol Danger but a Brand New Pleasure*. Urbana, IL: National Council of Teachers of English.

———. 2000. *Alice Walker in the Classroom: Living by the Word*. Urbana, IL: National Council of Teachers of English.

———. 2002. *Sandra Cisneros in the Classroom: Do Not Forget to Reach*. Urbana, IL: National Council of Teachers of English.

———. 2006. *Judith Ortiz Cofer in the Classroom: A Woman in Front of the Sun*. Urbana, IL: National Council of Teachers of English.

Jahren, Hope. 2017. *Lab Girl*. New York: Vintage.

Jarrow, Gail. 2015. *Fatal Fever: Tracking Down Typhoid Mary*. Honesdale, PA: Calkins Creek.

Jhabvala, Ruth Prawer. 2016. *Heat and Dust*. Berkeley, CA: Counterpoint.

Jiménez, Francisco. 1997. *The Circuit: Stories from the Life of a Migrant Child*. Albuquerque, NM: University of New Mexico Press.

Kakutani, Michiko. 2017. "Transcript: President Obama on What Books Mean to Him." *The New York Times*, January 16. www.nytimes.com/2017/01/16/books/transcript-president-obama-on-what-books-mean-to-him.html?mcubz=3.

Kalanithi, Paul. 2016. *When Breath Becomes Air*. New York: Random House.

Kingsolver, Barbara. 1998. *The Bean Trees*. New York: HarperCollins.

Konnikova, Maria. 2014. "Being a Better Online Reader." *The New Yorker*, July 16. www.newyorker.com/science/maria-konnikova/being-a-better-online-reader.

Lapham, Lewis. 2017. "Homo Faber." *Lapham's Quarterly* X (2): 13–21.

Lee, Harper. 1988. *To Kill a Mockingbird*. New York: Grand Central.

L'Engle, Madeline. 2012. *A Wrinkle in Time*. Anniversary ed. New York: Square Fish.

Lepore, Jill. 2017. "A Golden Age for Dystopian Fiction: What to Make of Our New Literature of Radical Pessimism." *The New Yorker*, June 5 and 12. www.newyorker.com/magazine/2017/06/05/a-golden-age-for-dystopian-fiction.

Levitin, Daniel. 2014. *The Organized Mind: Thinking Straight in the Age of Information Overload.* New York: Penguin.

Lewis, John, Andrew Aydin, and Nate Powell. 2016. *March: Book Three.* Marietta, GA: Top Shelf Productions.

Lin, Grace. 2011. *Where the Mountain Meets the Moon.* Boston: Little Brown.

Liu, Ziming. 2012. "Digital Reading." *Chinese Journal of Library and Information Science (English edition)* 5 (1): 85–94. http://scholarworks.sjsu.edu/cgi/viewcontent.cgi?article=1067&context=slis_pub.

Mann, Tracy. 2017. *Secrets from the Eating Lab.* New York: HarperCollins.

———. 2008. *Collected Stories.* New York: Harper.

———. 2014. *Love in the Time of Cholera.* New York: Vintage.

Marra, Anthony. 2014. *A Constellation of Vital Phenomena.* London: Hogarth.

———. 2016. *The Tsar of Love and Techno.* London: Hogarth.

Marrin, Albert. 2011. *Flesh and Blood So Cheap: The Triangle Fire and Its Legacy.* New York: Knopf.

Martel, Yann. 2002. *Life of Pi.* Boston: Houghton Mifflin Harcourt.

Martin, George R. R. 2011. *A Game of Thrones.* New York: Bantam.

Mathabane, Mark. 2011. *Kaffir Boy: The True Story of a Black Youth Coming of Age in Apartheid South Africa.* London: New Millennium Books.

McCarthy, Cormac. 2010. *Blood Meridian, or The Evening Redness in the West.* New York: Vintage.

Miller, Donalyn, with Susan Kelly. 2013. *Reading in the Wild: The Book Whisperer's Keys to Cultivating Lifelong Reading Habits.* San Francisco: Jossey-Bass.

Milton, John. 1896. *The Sonnets of John Milton.* Edited by Mark Pattison. New York: D. Appleton.

Montgomery, Sy, and Keith Ellenbogen. 2017. *Amazon Adventure: How Tiny Fish Are Saving the World's Largest Rainforest.* Boston: HMH.

Morrison, Toni. 2007a. *Beloved.* New York: Vintage.

———. 2007b. *Song of Solomon.* New York: Vintage.

Moss, Miriam. 2017. *Girl on a Plane*. Boston: HMH.

Murphy, Jim. 2014. *An American Plague: The True and Terrifying Story of the Yellow Fever Epidemic of 1793*. Boston: Clarion.

Myers, Walter Dean. 2011. *Riot*. New York: EgmontUSA.

Nabokov, Vladimir. 2010. *Lolita*. New York: Vintage.

National Center for Educational Statistics. 2018. https://nces.ed.gov/programs/coe /indicator_cgf.asp.

National Governors Association (NGA) Center for Best Practices and Council of Chief State School Officers (CCSSO). 2010. *Common Core State Standards for English Language Arts and Literacy in History/Social Studies, Science, and Technological Subjects*. Washington, DC: NGA Center and CCSSO. www.corestandards.org/the-standards.

NCS Pearson. 2014. *New York State Testing Program Grade 7 Common Core English Language Arts Test: Released Questions with Annotations*. Bloomington, MN: NCS Pearson. www.engageny.org/file/103116/download/2014_ela_grade_7_sample _annotated_items.pdf.

Neff, David, Richard F. Cohen, and Rick Korch. 1994. *The Football Encyclopedia: The Complete History of Professional Football from 1892 to the Present*. New York: St. Martin's.

Nelson, Marilyn. 2015. *My Seneca Village*. South Hampton, NH: Namelos.

Noah, Trevor. 2016. *Born a Crime: Stories from a South African Childhood*. New York: Spiegel and Grau.

Ntirkana, Jackson, and Wilson Meikuaya. 2016. *The Last Maasai Warriors: An Autobiography*. Toronto, ON: Me to We.

O'Brian, Patrick. 1990. *Master and Commander*. New York: W. W. Norton.

Orr, David. 2011. *Beautiful and Pointless: A Guide to Modern Poetry*. New York: HarperCollins.

Orwell, George. 1946. "Why I Write." *Gangrel* 4 (Summer): 5–10. http://orwell.ru /library/essays/wiw/english/e_wiw.

———. 1983. *1984*. Boston: Houghton Mifflin Harcourt.

Ottaviani, Jim, and Maris Wicks. 2015. *Primates: The Fearless Science of Jane Goodall, Dian Fosse, and Biruté Galdikas.* New York: Square Fish.

Park, Linda Sue. 2002. *A Single Shard.* Boston: HMH.

———. 2011. *A Long Walk to Water.* Boston: HMH.

Paulsen, Gary. 2011. *Woods Runner.* New York: Wendy Lamb Books.

Pawel, Miriam. 2015. *The Crusades of Cesar Chavez: A Biography.* New York: Bloomsbury.

Potter, Beatrix. 2012. "The Tale of the Flopsy Bunnies." In *Peter Rabbit and Other Stories.* Lit2Go edition. http://etc.usf.edu/lit2go/148/peter-rabbit-and-other-stories/4929/the-tale-of-the-flopsy-bunnies/.

Pulman, Philip. 2001. *The Golden Compass.* New York: Yearling.

Pynchon, Thomas. 2012. *The Crying of Lot 49.* New York: Penguin.

Radzinsky, Edvard. 1997. *Stalin.* New York: Anchor.

Rideout, Vicky. 2015. *The Common Sense Census: Media Use by Tweens and Teens.* San Francisco: Common Sense Media. www.commonsensemedia.org/sites/default/files/uploads/research/census_researchreport.pdf.

Rosen, Michael, and Quentin Blake. 2005. *Michael Rosen's Sad Book.* Somerville, MA: Candlewick.

Rosenblatt, Louise. 1983. *Literature as Exploration.* New York: Modern Language Association.

Rowling, J. K. 2017. *Harry Potter and the Philosopher's Stone.* London: Bloomsbury.

Sandel, Michael. 2010. *Justice: What's the Right Thing to Do?* New York: Farrar, Straus and Giroux.

Saramago, José. 1997. *Blindness.* New York: Harcourt Brace.

Schmoker, Michael. 1989. *Protocols of Reading.* New Haven, CT: Yale University Press.

———. 2017. "The Power of Focus." *Principal Leadership* 17 (3): 42–45.

Schwartz, Lynn Sharon. 2001. *Ruined by Reading: A Life in Books.* Boston: Beacon.

Shakespeare, William. 2003. *Macbeth.* New York: Simon and Schuster.

———. 2004. *Julius Caesar*. New York: Simon and Schuster.

Shanahan, Timothy, and Cynthia Shanahan. 2008. "Teaching Disciplinary Literacy to Adolescents: Rethinking Content-Area Literacy." *Harvard Educational Review* 78 (1): 40-59.

———. 2017. "Disciplinary Literacy: Just the FAQs." *Educational Leadership* 74 (5): 18–22.

Sheinkin, Steve. 2017. *Undefeated: Jim Thorpe and the Carlyle Indian School Football Team*. New York: Roaring Brook.

Shelley, Mary Wollstonecraft. 2008. *Frankenstein: or, the Modern Prometheus*. Project Guttenberg. www.gutenberg.org/files/84/84-h/84-h.htm.

Shetterly, Margot Lee. 2016. *Hidden Figures: The American Dream and the Untold Story of the Black Women Mathematicians Who Helped Win the Space Race*. New York: William Morrow.

Short, Deborah J., and Shannon Fitzsimmons. 2007. *Double the Work: Challenges and Solutions to Acquiring Language and Academic Literacy for Adolescent English Language Learners*. New York: Carnegie Corporation of New York.

Silko, Leslie Marmon. 2006. *Ceremony*. New York: Penguin Books.

Smith, Anna Deavere. 1993. *Fires in the Mirror*. New York: Anchor.

———. 1994. *Twilight: Los Angeles, 1992*. New York: Anchor.

Stanovich, K. 1986. "Matthew Effects in Reading: Some Consequences of Individual Differences in the Acquisition of Literacy." *Reading Research Quarterly* 21 (4): 360–407.

State of Illinois. 2017. *Illinois 2017 Rules of the Road*. Springfield, IL: State of Illinois.

Steinbeck, John. 2000. *The Pearl*. New York: Penguin.

Stelson, Carin. 2016. *Sachiko: A Nagasaki Bomb Survivor's Story*. Minneapolis, MN: Carolrhoda Books.

Stevenson, Harold W., and James W. Stigler. 1992. *The Learning Gap: Why Our Schools Are Failing and What We Can Learn from Japanese and Chinese Education*. New York: Summit Books.

Szymborska, Wisława. 1995. *View with a Grain of Sand*. New York: Harcourt Brace.

Tan, Amy. 2006. *The Joy Luck Club.* New York: Penguin.

Terkel, Studs. 1997. *Working: People Talk About What They Do All Day and How They Feel About What They Do.* New York: New Press.

———. 2005a. *American Dreams: Lost and Found.* New York: New Press.

———. 2005b. *Hard Times: An Oral History of the Great Depression.* New York: New Press.

———. 2006. *Division Street: America.* New York: New Press.

Thomas, Angie. 2017. *The Hate U Give.* New York: Balzer and Bray.

Tretheway, Natasha. 2012. *Beyond Katrina: A Meditation on the Mississippi Gulf Coast.* Athens, GA: University of Georgia Press.

Troupe, Quincy. 2002. *Transcircularities: New and Selected Poems.* Minneapolis, MN: Coffee House.

Turner, Brian. 2015. *My Life as a Foreign Country: A Memoir.* New York: W. W. Norton.

US Department of Education, Institute of Education Sciences, National Center for Education Statistics, National Assessment of Educational Progress (NAEP). 2009a. "Classroom Context: Class Reading Discussion." The Nation's Report Card. www.nationsreportcard.gov/reading_2009/context _4.aspx?tab_id=tab2&subtab_id=Tab_1#tabsContainer.

———. 2009b. "Classroom Context: Number of Pages Read." The Nation's Report Card. https://nationsreportcard.gov/reading_2009/context_2 .aspx?tab_id=tab2&subtab_id=Tab_1#tabsContainter.

———. 2009c. "Classroom Context: Reading for Fun." The Nation's Report Card. www.nationsreportcard.gov/reading_2009/context _3.aspx?tab_id=tab2&subtab_id=Tab_1#tabsContainer.

US Department of Education, National Center for Education Statistics. 2015. "Local Education Agency Universe Survey." https://nces.ed.gov/programs /coe/indicator_cgf.asp.

Wiesel, Elie. 2006. *Night.* New York: Hill and Wang.

Wiesner, David, and Donna Jo Napoli. 2017. *Fish Girl.* Boston: Clarion.

Williams, Terry Tempest. 2016. *The Hour of Land: A Personal Topography of America's National Parks.* New York: Sarah Crichton Books.

Williams, William Carlos. 1962. *Asphodel, That Greeny Flower.* New York: New Directions Publishing Corporation.

Wilson, August. 1990. *The Piano Lesson.* New York: Plume.

Wineburg, Sam. 2015. "Why Historical Thinking Is Not About History." *History News* 72 (2): 13–16. https://stacks.stanford.edu/file/druid:yy383km0067/Wineburg%20Hist.%20Thinking%20is%20not%20about%20history.pdf.

Winthrop, Elizabeth. 2007. *Counting on Grace.* New York: Yearling.

Winton, Tim. 2017. *Island Home: A Landscape Memoir.* Minneapolis, MN: Milkweed Editions.

Woodson, Jacqueline. 2016. *Brown Girl Dreaming.* New York: Puffin Books.

Wordsworth, William. 1998. *The Collected Poems of William Wordsworth.* London: Wordsworth Editions Ltd.

Wright, Richard. 2007. *Black Boy: A Record of Childhood and Youth.* New York: HarperCollins.

Zehr, Mary Ann. 2010. "Well-Known ELL Expert Says Simplified Texts Are a Problem." *Learning the Language* (blog), September 30. http://blogs.edweek.org/edweek/learning-the-language/2010/09/lily-wong_fillmore_simplified.html.